Quantum Anthropologies

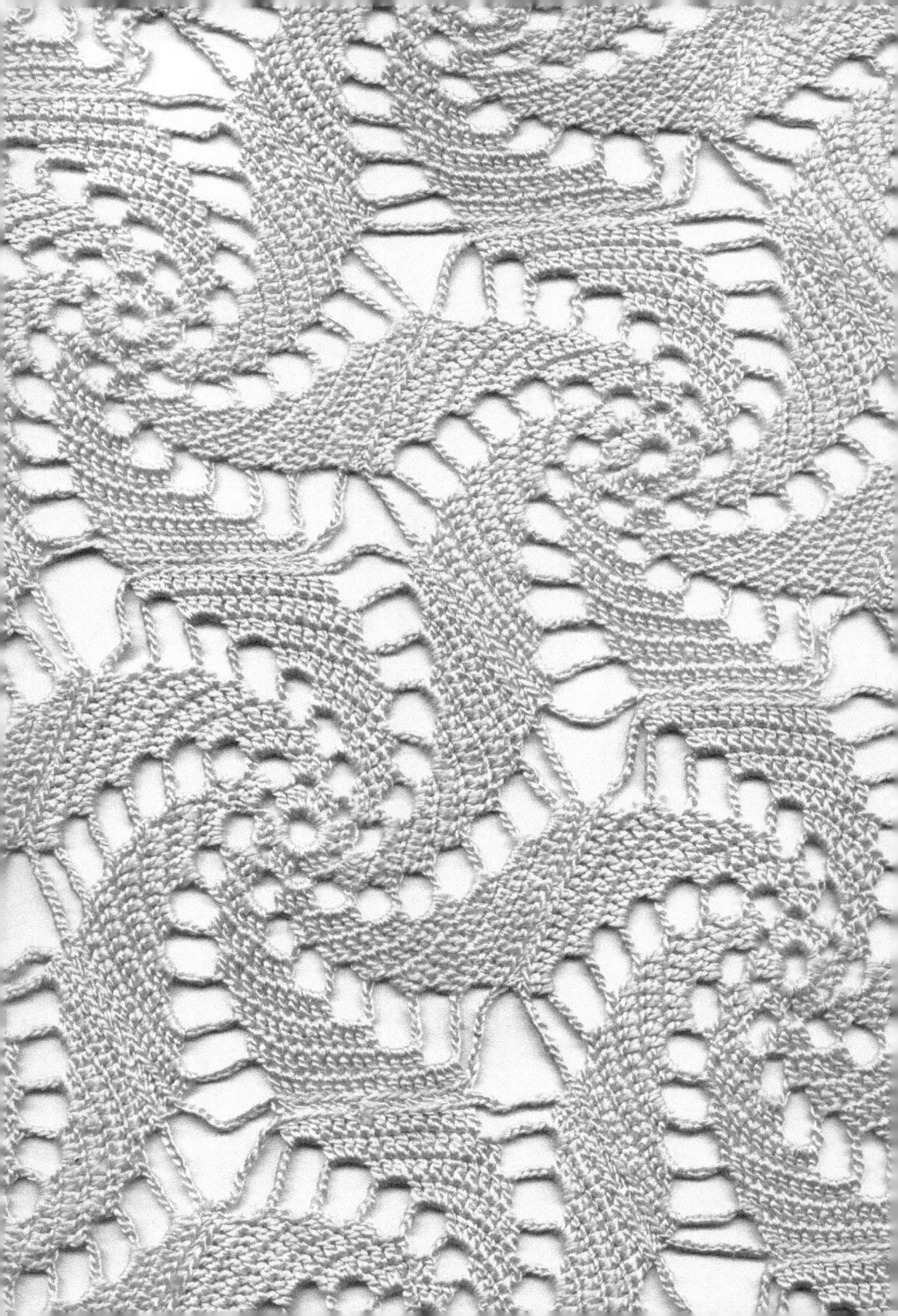

Vicki Kirby

Quantum Anthropologies

Life at Large

Duke University Press

Durham and London

2011

Designed by C. H. Westmoreland
Typeset in Warnock Pro by Keystone Typesetting, Inc.
Library of Congress Cataloging-in-Publication Data appear on the last
printed page of this book.

Frontispiece: needlework by Claudia Vigeant

Contents

Preface

The Question of Supplementarity
—A Quantum Problematic

As I collect my thoughts about what it is that gives my work its special signature, a signature where "points in the pattern" of its argumentation reveal a certain focus, an attention, or even obsession about something whose relevance may well seem obscure, I recall a scene in Berlin nearly two years ago. I had presented a paper that in preliminary fashion considered Derrida's work on the question of the a-human and genetics, and although my questioner registered no disquiet with the general direction of my argument it was clear that he had a problem with my vocabulary. "Writing," "textuality," "language in the general sense"? Given that I was engaging questions of life, science, biology, and system, why was I still wedded to Derridean terms? I was aware at the time that I answered the question poorly, and so I continued to be bothered about what I could have said that might have explained why I was determined not to "move on," or more to the point, why "moving on" demanded that I stubbornly stay put. The same uneasiness with my working frame of reference, or what was perceived as its obvious limitations, came up again a few months ago in a different guise. In this instance it was the relevance of Ferdinand de Saussure's work for computational or neurological analysis, which was deemed, quite simply, obsolete: surely we need contemporary theorists to engage contemporary technological and scientific complexities, and moreover, theories that specifically address the subject matter under review?

These are the sorts of prejudices, seemingly reasonable and straightforward, that the arguments in the following chapters hope to trouble. Although the proper name Derrida isn't always foregrounded and may sometimes even appear absent, my own reading of the legacy of deconstruction is always at work. By taking Derrida's notion of an "open system" to its logical conclusion, the senses of particularism—whether individual subjects, objects, words, methodologies, or even systems—lose their identifying outlines as entities or atomic individuations that communicate, or relate to each other, with causal effect. Instead they can be read as different expressions of the same phenomenon. A consequence of this condensation, this concretion or *différance*, is that grammatology becomes a "positive science" for Derrida. But what does this mean, and why, to my mind, does it represent such an extraordinary challenge that its implications go unnoticed, confined as they are to disciplinary argument within philosophy and literature? For Derrida reminds us that "the concept of text or of context which guides me embraces and does not exclude the world, reality, history. . . . [T]he text is not the book, it is not confined in a volume itself confined to the library. It does not suspend reference. . . . *Différance* is a reference and vice versa" (1988, 137).

Because the reasoning that obstructs the taking up of these implications is eloquently exemplified in John Protevi's *Political Physics* (2001), and because Protevi's sympathetic assessment of deconstruction's strengths, but also of its inadequacies, is widely held, his argument provides an instructive touchstone for situating my own contribution to questions of matter and indeed, a political physics, and a ready introduction to what follows in the rest of the book.

In regard to matters of substance and science—pragmatics and physical reality, those "convergent fields assuming the highest importance in the material structuring of the current global system of bodies politic: recombinant genetics, cognitive science, dynamical systems theories and others" (2001, 2)—Protevi is convinced that deconstruction can have little to say. He even cites Alan Sokal and Jean Bricmont from the "science wars" to buttress this perception, for they do ultimately "absolve Derrida of most of the culpability in overstepping the philosophy/science border they impute to others: 'since there is no systematic misuse of (or indeed attention to) science in Derrida's work'" (2001, 5).

However, it would be unfair to say that Protevi fails to appreciate the value of Derrida's contribution or that his reading has no accepted validity (there are many Derridas!), for his endorsement of the philosopher is exuberant. Derrida is a "fantastic reader of the history of philosophy, a master at showing the breakdown of philosophy's pretensions to self-grounding. . . . [H]is reading techniques, his scrupulous attention to detail, are a welcome addition to any philosopher's toolkit: these cannot be forgotten and retain their usefulness in many, but not all, contexts" (2001, 6). In sum, Derrida's interventions are persuasively "fantastic" and pragmatically relevant if they remain confined to a very restricted understanding of language, ideation, and culture that Derrida himself was, at least most of the time, at pains to reject.

What is at stake in this assumption that deconstruction can only prove useful if its implications are contained? What happens if we acknowledge and elaborate Derrida's insights, granting an even greater operationalism to what is sometimes preliminary in his thought? For example, the consequences of Derrida's own arguments about the problematic of grounding must be read as precious nonsense if, having digested them, Protevi can blithely describe materiality (Nature) as "something" to be added to conceptuality (Culture). What is the point, *really*, in championing the difficult convolutions of deconstructive thought as well as feminist and other political interventions that question the disjunction of the human from the nonhuman, or mind (culture) from body (nature), if this same disjunction remains the true and inescapable ground of our arguments? And even if we were to concede that this disjunction was a reality, how then can these separate systems relate or communicate their radical and unrepresentable (incommunicable) difference? I would like to think that deconstruction cannot be enlisted to persuade us that such questions can be put aside.

When Derrida reminds his audience that deconstruction's implications could not be confined to philosophy any more than they could be restricted between the covers of a book, perhaps the most provocative consequence of such clarifications is that the reader/writer of this "general text" is necessarily dispersed—it is not located, at least not in any classical sense, in a human agent. Within this "open system" whose only constant is mutation/writing, the same questions that are confronted in the physical sciences about determination, agency, causality, space-time involvement, and "spooky" entanglement, are all operative. Importantly, dispersing literacy (textuality) as the weaving of life itself means not only that "old" texts remain contemporary and productively alive because never closed off in a past that is simply behind us, but also that the "texts" of seemingly pri-meval organisms, or even a supposedly inanimate and lifeless entity such as a photon, become subjects of cognitive and agential entanglement and observational intention.

My own intervention throughout these chapters is to recast the question of the anthropological—the human—in a more profound and destabilizing way than its disciplinary frame of reference will allow. And I have done this by reading Derrida's "no outside of text" and the sense of systemic involve-ment to which it attests, as "no outside of Nature." Such a reading will not affirm Protevi's understanding of deconstruction as a methodology whose ultimate goal is to muddle conceptual integrity and to underline the com-plexity of the human condition's representational solipsism (Culture). As Protevi represents deconstruction's goals, "The general text, as we will see, while inextricably binding force and signification in 'making sense,' is not an engagement with matter itself; such an engagement is impossible for deconstruction, for which 'matter' remains a concept, a philosopheme to be read in the text of metaphysics, or functions as a marker of a radical alterity outside the oppositions that make up the text of metaphysics" (2001, 19).

While there is much in Protevi's overall argument to be commended, and I am not disputing his scholarship, it is important to underline that his assumption that Derrida's "no outside metaphysics" *must* exclude matter, that matter is incapable of representing itself, entirely misses the extraordi-nary puzzle of how a system's apparent interiority can incorporate what appears to be separate and different, or indeed, nonlocal. Whereas "text" and "metaphysics" are sites of excavation, discovery, and reinvention for Derrida, Protevi uncritically embraces their *received* meanings, as did my interlocutors above.

Derrida's work on supplementarity can certainly be read as a convoluted argument about the impossibility of escaping metaphysics (ideation/the concept), but it can also be interpreted as an acknowledgment of the self-involvements of a meta-*physis* whose *internal* torsions have quantum im-plications. My interest is in a more robust exploration of the latter rather than a corrective that will return us to a reworked, if conventional under-standing of metaphysics/conception as something that is utterly different from matter/substance: the enclosed domain that guarantees human ex-ceptionalism. The naiveté that refuses the *question* of matter, here also, the *question* of language, by simply adding their presumed differences together marks a lack of rigor whose complacency appears time and again when the puzzle of relationality, difference, and implication is "resolved" through terms that evoke conjunction, aggregation, assemblage, and connection.

The target of my own intervention is this simple sense of "and" that necessarily recuperates an uncritical understanding of identity even as it claims to interrogate it. And here we conjure with the quantum resonance of Derrida's insights that refuse to supplement identity, and instead, open the text, or any individual identification, to an interiority whose articulating energy is the entire system. This expansive sense of interiority is the most difficult to think because thinking presumes cuts and divisions of simple separation, whereas these are, as Karen Barad explains it, ontoepistemological entanglements (2007, 185). Attesting to the difficulty, Derrida expresses his impatience with explaining the spatial and temporal complications in his arguments in terms of a continuum, an interpretation that for him is "worse than sleepwalking" and "scatterbrained" (2002, 398). The scene of writing and its generality is not a "field" that is appropriately enormous because it must comprehend and include everything. The real paradox here that refigures the sense of quantum scale (the preconception that entanglement is only operative at the micro-level), is that there is no "everything" that preexists the relationality that *is* the scene of writing, the scene of ontological genesis as enfolding. For this reason the "entire scene" is already rehearsed and actively present in any and every "atom" of its instantiation/individuation.

Perhaps I can conclude this little introductory guide by suggesting that if the quantum implications of what we do in the humanities and social sciences is not an idle metaphor, then intertextuality suggests that in some quite uncanny sense, so-called cultural critics are already practicing science—we really are in the business of material production. The argument I am trying to make is that the investment in the identity of the limit, a limit that separates human exceptionalism (with its cultural misrepresentations) from the substantive reality that it can't know and can't be, has prevented us from appreciating that our corporeal realities and their productive iterations *are* material reinventions. Life reads and rewrites itself, and this operation of universal genesis and reproduction is even internal to the tiny marks on this page, which are effective transubstantiations.

In the following argument I would like to persuade my reader, contra

Derrida but perhaps not entirely, that the grammatological textile, which is never not worldly, is in reality *already* present within the covers of a book. What do we forfeit and what do we gain in claiming Nature's "textuality," its literacy, as our own?

Acknowledgments

A considerable part of this project's thinking and writing time was funded by an Australian Research Council Discovery Grant (2006–9), which also facilitated conference and research travel. I also received a Research Promotion Grant from the University of New South Wales to assist with the final stages of the book's compilation.

As this project covers quite a few years I owe a debt to an international band of supporters who have at various times encouraged the direction of my research and provided professional guidance and opportunity and always friendly good cheer. I am grateful to Heather Worth, Gail Weiss, Penny Deutscher, Sha Xin Wei, Anna Yeatman, Prafulla Kar, Patricia Ticineto Clough, Gary Dowsett, Mariam Fraser, Myra Hird, Susan Squier, Lilyan White, Michal Reed, Anna Bennett, and, more recently, Nicole Vitellone, Peta Hinton, and Florence Chiew.

I would also like to acknowledge my graduate student cohort. Because the Australian postgraduate system has no coursework, the supervisory relationship is one-on-one and extremely intense in its intellectual exchange and commitment. I am privileged to have supervised such a stellar group of young scholars, many of them national award winners and medalists, and I am sure my work has been improved by this environment.

Some colleagues deserve special mention. I have enjoyed the intellectual company over the years of the remarkable polymath Tom Lamarre. A mine of weird and wonderful references, he is never afraid to entertain their wildest consequences. My good friend Liz Wilson has been a stalwart supporter, providing hands-on assistance and encouragement with every aspect of my career, facilitating professional connections, reading drafts of chapters, and offering excellent advice when things proved difficult. More recently, my happy encounters with Karen Barad have been inspiring. I regard her scholarship and generosity in "throwing it around" with me as nothing short of exhilarating. In the revisions of these chapters the influence of *Meeting the Universe Halfway* (2007) will certainly be in evidence.

I would also like to thank Vigo Ruja for "making everything good" for as long as he could, and Wayne Mason for the structure, consistency, and decency of our relationship. My mother, Pat Kirby, an octogenarian who still has more energy than I do, continues to spend quite a bit of it on motherly ministrations that are greatly appreciated. And last but not least, I want to thank Judi Ruja for being such a reliable and unwavering compass in my life over the last few years.

Versions of these chapters have been published previously, but all appear here in much revised and often considerably expanded form. "Quantum Anthropologies: Life at Large," originally published as "Quantum Anthropologies," in *Derrida Downunder*, edited by L. Simmons and H. Worth (Palmerston North: Dunmore Press, 2001), 53–68, © reverted to author; "Just Figures?: Forensic Clairvoyance, Mathematics, and the Language Question," originally published in *SubStance* 35, no. 107, part 2 (2005): 1–24, © 2005 by the Board of Regents of the University of Wisconsin System, reproduced courtesy of the University of Wisconsin Press; "Enumerating Language: 'The Unreasonable Effectiveness of Mathematics,'" originally published in *Configurations: Journal of Literature, Science and Technology* 12, no. 3 (Fall 2004): 417–39, reprinted with permission from The Johns Hopkins University Press; "Natural Convers(at)ions: Or, What If Culture Was Really Nature All Along?," originally published in *Material Feminisms*, edited by Susan J. Hekman and Stacy Alaimo (Bloomington: Indiana University Press, 2008), 214–36, reproduced with permission from Indiana University Press; "(Con)founding 'the Human': Incestuous Beginnings," originally published as "(Con)founding 'the Human': Incestuous Beginnings," in *Queering the Non/Human*, edited by Noreen Giffney and Myra J. Hird (Aldershot, U.K.: Ashgate Press, 2008), 35–54, reproduced with permission from Ashgate Press; "Culpability and the Double-Cross: Irigaray with Merleau-Ponty," originally published in *Feminist Interpretations of Maurice Merleau-Ponty*, edited by D. Olkowski and G. Weiss (University Park: Pennsylvania State University Press, 2006), 127–45, reproduced with permission from Pennsylvania State University Press.

1. Anthropology Diffracted

Originary Humanicity

As deconstruction aims to shake up the routine logic through which we conceptualize the world and our place in it, it is not surprising that all the different manifestations of the deconstructive enterprise show a special fascination with the notion of beginnings. Deconstruction scrutinizes the foundations of an argument, or what appears so firmly established that it requires no justification, because its fixation with origins uncovers their peculiar capacity for innovation, endurance, and even ubiquity. The suggestion that a beginning has something of a mutating existence tests our comprehension in a most fundamental way, for it seems only natural to think of an origin as a fixed and discrete event, captured forever in the aspic of one particular place and time. After all, we require initializing coordinates in order to discriminate one thing from another, attribute causal explanations, or arrive at even the most basic decisions and evaluations in our personal and public lives. We simply can't assume a sense of self or hope to understand the world without them.

Although a deconstructive practice will certainly concede this necessity, these causal moments of initiation that also presume a terminus will suffer a dimensional collapse nevertheless. And yet the complexity here is that the origin's existence isn't snuffed out by this contraction, nor is the particular intensity of its energy diminished. It is more a case of trying to refine and elaborate the rather frugal conventions of measurement and comprehension through which we confer existence, hoping that an exuberance of fractal dimension might emerge. How else can we apprehend the immensity that is accommodated within the instant?

Geoffrey Bennington, a writer who seems quite at home in these paradoxical spaces, notes that deconstruction's obsession with beginnings can have "scandalous" outcomes. Bennington draws on salient references from the Derridean opus to remind us that the origin incorporates myriad related questions, whose erratic provenance is simply "unacceptable" and even "ridiculous" in traditional philosophical circles. After all, deconstruction conjures with "an absolute past that has never been present . . . an originary repetition . . . a finite infinite . . . a supplement which 'produces' what it supplements." And as if that wasn't enough, it also insists that "perception does not exist . . . that the proper name cannot be proper . . . that the *cogito* is mad errancy . . . that there is nothing outside the text . . . that in the beginning was the telephone, [and] that I am perhaps dead" (Derrida and Bennington 1993, 18–19).

It is not surprising that curiosity about deconstruction's more scandalous aphorisms has been diminished, and even dissolved, by years of repetition. How many students and teachers of contemporary critical analysis for example, would today experience consternation, alarm, or even wonder, upon hearing Bennington's list of improbable conclusions? A more likely response is to disengage from the peculiar and especially challenging conundrums of deconstruction by interpreting them as *signs of a particular style* of literary and cultural criticism or philosophical methodology (albeit the methodology of those who eschew methodology). As a result, these difficulties become the identifying signature of a certain school of criticism rather than provocations for an urgent reassessment of how we comprehend reality. Thus, the more successfully deconstruction problematizes the origin and with it a battery of companion notions such as causality, identity, temporality, and so on, the more the intransigence of these "concepts" is demonstrated and deconstruction's own identity is affirmed as "the theory that does that."

On first glance it appears that the perverse existence of the origin, with its obstinate persistence and yet playful errancy, is not a mistake that can be corrected. And perhaps it is for this reason that the actual implications of opening the origin to a past that has yet to arrive simply can't be taken seriously. We would be unlikely to say, for example, that things are *naturally* this ambiguous, that the ontological weight, or "hereness" of an entity, could have no location (nonlocality), or to put this another way, that the trace of an entity's "being-itself" could be present in various and seemingly separate locations. Indeed, evidence of an object's ubiquity or the mutability of its definition is regarded as incontrovertible proof that this existential perversity can be explained and, as we will see, thereby denied or put aside. The insistence that ontological complexity is merely apparent, that it is an attribute of Culture's operations, or that its anomalous signature has a human author, is an attempt to hold the line on a more radical, or certainly more disturbing, investigation of what we mean by identity and causality. Within contemporary critical analysis, the accepted way to deal with this threatened meltdown is to attribute these complications to the vagaries and conundrums of language, and to insist that it is not the object itself that is under scrutiny but "the discursive effect" of the object's mediation. Thus natural determinations assumed to be rigid, prescriptive, and capable of extinguishing any puny appeal to individual or social agency are replaced by cultural determinations that are regarded as plastic, contestable, and able to invite intervention and reconstitution.

It is this style of postmodern criticism and its permutations that I want to interrogate, that is, those approaches that interpret the self-referentiality of language as the constitutive self-enclosure of Culture. However, in anticipation that my imagined reader is sympathetic to the general reasoning behind cultural constructionist arguments and their successful assault on a conservative humanism—in short, the assumption that individuals have an autonomy that guarantees agency and intention as rightly theirs; that they are self-aware and therefore responsible for their own thoughts and actions—I can only reassure such a reader that it is far from my intention to repudiate the importance and complexity of these arguments. On the contrary, my dilemma is that I am entirely persuaded by the value of the work that I address; indeed, so much so that I think the direction of its interventions and insights have far greater reach than has yet been conceded.

My task then is to try to explain why I regard current understandings of "language," even those that derive from the canon of postmodern and poststructural criticism, as restricted; and further, why these same arguments, viewed from another perspective, might be said to have scientific and quantum implications. The sheer exorbitance of these implications makes them difficult to work with because one can't decide in advance whether they can *usefully* be enlisted into current ways of determining and resolving political and ethical quandaries. My conviction, however, is that our inability to contain these difficulties and accommodate them within current management strategies opens the question of use and political pragmatism to something that is easily censored, by definition.

The need to control and thereby deny difficulty is certainly not new. To mention just one example, the bizarre aspects of atomic identity and determination in physics tend to be handled in a similar way by most of us. Although we may believe, as quantum science indicates, that the nature of physical reality exceeds our everyday perceptions in quite fantastic ways, we tend to rationalize the discrepancy by attributing complexity to a particular arena of research and scholarship, as if the arcane nature of these findings is quite irrelevant to the stuff of the quotidian. Even among the physics community this same attempt to ignore the most astonishing implications of quantum relations was maintained even as the empirical evidence for their plausibility (Bell's inequalities) began appearing in 1964.[1] On this last point, Karen Barad comments, "Considering the profundity of Bell's theorem, it is an interesting sociological fact that for many years after its publication scant attention was paid to this result.... It is difficult not to read this as a measure of the lack of interest in foundational issues in quantum theory in a resolutely neo-positivist period" (2007, 291).[2] Another argument that discourages curiosity about the possible relationship between everyday life and quantum relations is the received wisdom that the minute scale of quantum behavior can have no application in the macroscopic world of human affairs. Again, Barad explains that although such behaviors are not readily discernible they are nevertheless operative and have sometimes been observed, such that "the question of macroscopic quantum states is not an idle matter" (2007, 270). Given an apparent need to quarantine the ordinary fabric of life, and importantly, how we think about it, from any troublesome complication, it is not surprising that the compass of deconstructive criticism is also quite small, confined to only a few disciplinary locations within the humanities and even there, appearing more like a historical curiosity than a viable contemporary challenge.

Despite the extraordinary scope of Derrida's achievement, it has found a familiar home in those disciplines that profess special expertise in studying the vagaries of rhetoric, textuality, discourse, and representation; in sum, language itself. However, given that "language itself" in the Derridean corpus involves a generalized displacement of the way we conventionally think about language, there is something disturbing about the utter predictability of this localized accommodation. My interest here, however, is not one of broadening the purchase of deconstruction as if the inclusion of architecture, law, history, or a battery of other disciplinary formations might answer this sense of restriction. After all, these particular disciplines have already addressed and significantly elaborated deconstruction's relevance.[3] My aim, rather, is to interrupt the complacency with which we view "language" in all its forms, because even in the disparate areas of inquiry that concede the textual or informational nature of their disciplinary objects the notion of language is merely extended to accommodate different media, different genres of representation, or different behaviors whose metaphoric resonance with language structures is acknowledged but not explained. Derrida informs us, however, that deconstruction is not a methodology: it is not a procedural set of maneuvers, an application or template of inquiry through which an alien object might be ciphered. Nor can its implications be subordinated to the philosophical dialectic, whether Hegelian or Platonic, that pursues the self-experience of thought where truth promises to emerge as the accurate resolution of self-reflection. In other words, a Derridean intervention is not reducible to the Concept, at least not in any orthodox sense of what we might mean by this.

Derrida's *"point de méthode"* (point/lack of method) (1981a, 271), then, is not compatible with the circumscribed aims of philosophy proper—"the closure of philosophy" in its disciplinary form, as Derrida calls it (2001, 114)—nor is its "object" simply contained within what we conventionally call representational systems of whatever stripe. Making a similar point, Rodolphe Gasché, one of deconstruction's most erudite and careful commentators, makes the provocative claim that "deconstruction is never the effect of a subjective act of desire or will or wishing. What provokes a deconstruction is rather of an 'objective' nature. It is a 'must' so to speak" (1986, 123). Although Gasché is certainly not reverting to any sense of scientific instrumentalism here, noting that "deconstruction, as a methodical principle, cannot be mistaken for anything resembling scientific procedural rules" (123), his comments remind us that deconstruction is difficult to place.

Deconstruction can certainly appear to adopt a meta-position in relation to its object, a gesture that seems compatible with the instrumentalism of scientific methodologies and claims to objectivity. Indeed, we might remember that Derrida's earliest attempts to explicate the difficulty of his project actually consider grammatology as a positive science. In the particular chapter in *Of Grammatology* that explores this question, Derrida concludes, "The constitution of a science or a philosophy of writing is a necessary and difficult task" (1984, 93). And in answer to Julia Kristeva's question in *Positions*, "To what extent is or is not grammatology a 'science?,'" Derrida refuses to reject the term. "Grammatology must pursue and consolidate whatever, in scientific practice, has always already begun to exceed the logocentric closure. This is why there is no simple answer to the question of whether grammatology is a 'science'" (1981b, 35–36).

If Derrida's "double-science" encourages us to "understand this *incompetence* of science which is also the incompetence of philosophy" (Derrida 1984, 93), then perhaps deconstruction's home is as uncomfortable yet essential to the sciences as it is to the humanities. Certainly, its *point de méthode* is not *a distinct analytical approach* with a definite object and limited disciplinary application. To put this differently and perhaps too obtusely at this stage, deconstruction need not assume that the object that emerges is simply an interpret*ed* object, a discursive *effect*, a *cultural* product—as if the reality of its identity is the meaning bestowed by an individual or collective (human) subject. In the rest of this discussion I will attempt to unpack this rather opaque assertion by looking at a fragment of Derrida's earliest work that reinvigorates the terms of the debate about the nature of reality, representation, and even truth.

Before doing this however, it might be helpful if I explain my own appreciation of what Derrida might be trying to evoke by his disclaimer about methodology that nevertheless insists on rigor and precision. The history of my particular intrigue with questions of language, and deconstruction in particular, rests on the marvelous contradiction that attends two of Ferdinand de Saussure's most well-known assertions; namely, his insistence on the arbitrary nature of the sign and his equally forceful assertion that a sign can only make sense because a *system* of signs gives it expression.[4] The tension here is that a system involves a relational coherence—an interdependency of some sort—and this relational binding is something we might define "the arbitrary" against. If we say that a system's internal coherence of what is *necessary* to its identity as *this* particular system (of language, for example) and not that system (of ecological processes, perhaps), then the decision that something is arbitrary must refer outside the system to secure this determination. However, the difference between what is internal and necessary to the system and what is external and independent of the system must remain *within* language as Saussure defines it—"in language there are only differences" (1981, 120) and "language is a system of pure values which are determined by nothing except the momentary arrangement of its terms" (80). Language cannot take its measure from anything that isn't language because it lacks positive terms and can only refer to itself.

This potential exorbitance of language and its overarching comprehension certainly exercised Saussure's thoughts, leading him to acknowledge that linguistics was not the master template through which the world was given reference and value. *"A science that studies the life of signs within society* is conceivable . . . I shall call it *semiology.* . . . Semiology would show what constitutes signs, what laws govern them. Since the science does not yet exist, no one can say what it would be; but it has a right to existence, a place staked out in advance. Linguistics is only a part of the general science of semiology; the laws discovered by semiology will be applicable to linguistics, and the latter will circumscribe a well-defined area within the mass of anthropological facts" (1981, 16).

In one tiny sentence that captures the energy of deconstruction's provocation, the now canonical assertion that *"there is nothing outside of the text"* (Derrida 1984, 158), the science of semiology is born as grammatology. However, whereas semiology envisaged an aggregation or assemblage of different systems that would somehow communicate with each other across the distance that identified them as separate, grammatology regards these different "entities" as articulations *of* the system. In other words, their respective identities are what we might describe as "mutualities" with no simple independence, and where their difference involves no distance at all. If these different systems do not preexist the communication that might pass between them, then the very notion of communication requires review.

At least for now, we can understand why Derrida might refuse to describe deconstruction as a methodology in any conventional sense, because grammatology begins with the assumption that the difference between the interpreter, the interpreting apparatus, as well as the difference between the object or concept under investigation, is compromised. Method cannot be an operational instrument of determination (making the causal decision about where to cut, where to delineate, where to merge) because the *entire* scene or system is actively involved in its own decipherment. According to deconstruction, differences are cut from the same cloth—they are all of a piece. This means that a deconstructive methodology is a mired business, *of necessity*, and one whose insights must follow rigorous protocols in order to demonstrate the complex nature and incisiveness of its practice. Importantly, the sense of textual *play* that accompanies these determinations is not capricious: it is not the case that anything goes.

Given the comprehensiveness of the grammatological textile it should be no surprise that deconstruction discovers itself in enterprises such as cybernetics, biology, and chemistry. Yet it is precisely here, at this point of *re-marking* these particular enterprises and their objects as expressions of textuality, that the *question* of language has been answered too quickly and thus inadvertently censored. Derrida's own explanation of deconstruction's ubiquity explicitly noted its manifestation "in other determined fields (mathematical and logical formalization, linguistics, ethnology, psychoanalysis, political economy, biology, the technology of information, programming, etc.)" (1981b, 7). However, the breadth of this universal conversation is routinely explained by attributing its resonance to the originating structures that are thought to give it form, namely, the linguistic and other cultural representations considered peculiar to human decipherment. Even cybernetic concessions to Nature's feedback loops and informational literacies will tend to bog down in communication models about informational relays, and a reiteration of the same problem, the hiving off of data from a material support.[5]

Derrida explicitly warned against this conflation of a "general textuality" with the reaffirmation of cultural mediation, that is, "the definition of a new self-interiority, a new 'idealism' if you will, of the text" (Derrida 1981b, 66). With the privileging of form over substance by Saussure we can understand why grammatology is commonly equated with information, and information with the unique abstraction of human invention that we call language, or why information theories tend to recuperate this division as information versus its support (complexity contra simplicity, or language defined against what is not language). Perhaps more insidiously, in the simple logic of identification that separates one system from another, Derrida's notion that differencing *is* "language" and that there is no outside this genetic involvement—that this involvement *is* the grammatological textile in all its expressions—is entirely lost. However, from another perspective, one that opens the identity of human species-being *through* the question of "language in the general sense," as well as the identity of information itself, we note that both humanism and antihumanism appear very similar. But what anxiety is being managed in this shared commitment to human identity and its unique capacities?

I am going to approach this question again by recounting two quite simple stories, each of which underlines my enduring curiosity about the ontology of language—systems of becoming whose relational imbrications do not separate out into ideality plus substance. Imagine this scene, which took place about twenty years ago, when I was first finding my way into the maze of the language question. I was waiting in line with a small group of scholarship recipients, each of us charged with the task of explaining our various intellectual projects to an assembled association of benefactors. I had been called upon to justify my enthusiasm for deconstructive criticism to a non-academic audience that, quite properly, expected to hear it was getting value for its investment. Needless to say I was somewhat apprehensive about my ability to convince them; I knew it would appear an esoteric and abstract form of research, with no pragmatic relevance whatsoever. And yet as it happened, and with no particular fuss or fanfare, the young biologist who spoke before me conveyed the peculiar stuff of my question with eloquent simplicity. The object of her special passion was the stingray, and as I recall, her interest in how cells talk to their neighbors was facilitated by the ease of observation that the larger neuronal structures of these particular creatures enabled. Despite these advantages however, her research team's empirical observations had revealed something entirely maddening about neuronal chatter. Her fascinated listeners were informed that receptor cells, which operate like locks that can only be opened by the right key or message, seemed possessed of some mysterious clairvoyance. They are able to anticipate when a message, which has yet to arrive, will have been addressed specifically to them, for the specific cells that *will be* involved unlock themselves in readiness. It is as if the identity and behavior of any *one* observable receptor cell is somehow stretched, or disseminated, in a space-time enfolding; as if they are located here, and yet also there, at the same time. But if the separation between sender and receiver is strangely compromised in this biological example, so too is the status of the message. To consider this more carefully, if the interval between the two is no distance at all, then what difference could a message effect, and what would it be? Strange stuff, this action at a distance that confounds the logic of origins and causality, and what we mean by identity as something separate in space and time.

I had, of course, heard it all before. Indeed, with some amusement I could see that the entangled identity of *one* cell within another had even assumed human proportions as we stood there in line, waiting to explain what made our individual research unique. Was this biologist already in receipt of my intellectual labors before our meeting, even as I tried to articulate the results that she, of course, had inevitably discovered? What infectious algorithm had already brought us together before our actual meeting?[6]

And now another story that may at first seem very distant from the language games of molecular biology—the behavior of lightning. As I live in something of an aerie whose panorama includes a significant sweep of the Sydney harbor and skyline, it is common to see electrical storms arcing across the city. As I've waited for the next flash, trying to anticipate where it might strike, I've wondered about the erratic logic of this fiery charge whose intent seems as capricious as it is determined. The assumption that lightning does exhibit a certain logic is evident in the common wisdom that lightning never strikes in the same place twice. But as Martin Uman, one of lightning's foremost interpreters tells us, the situation is quite the opposite. "Much of what is known about lightning today has been discovered precisely because lightning *does* strike the same structure over and over again. . . . The Empire State Building in New York City is struck by lightning an average of about 23 times a year. As many as 48 strikes have been recorded in one year, and during one thunderstorm eight strikes occurred within 24 minutes" (Uman 1986, 47).

Reading about electricity's predilection for tall buildings, lone trees on golf courses, tractors, and bodies of open water, I also learned that quite curious initiation rights precede these electrical encounters. An intriguing communication, a sort of stuttering chatter between the ground and the sky, appears to anticipate the actual stroke. A quite spectacular example is the phenomenon of St. Elmo's fire, a visible light show that can sometimes be seen to enliven an object in the moment, *just before the moment*, of the strike. If the communicative charge in this electrical recognition is certainly mysterious, my attempts to discover a satisfactory explanation for this mutual attraction have led me into a familiar labyrinth.

But let's begin with something whose behavior we might expect to be significantly more straightforward than the contentious nature of St. Elmo's fire and its associations with those "mobile luminous spheres" called ball lightning.[7] For example, if we begin by considering a lightning stroke, the flash that we are used to observing in an electrical storm, we will probably assume that it originates in a cloud and is then discharged in the direction of the ground. However, if this directional causality were true, it would be reasonable to ask how lightning can be apprised of its most economical route to the earth before it has been tested. According to experts, the path of lightning is one of arcing disjuncture that runs in both an upward and downward direction (Uman 1986, 73). Buildings and other objects on the ground can initiate strikes by sending out what are called upward moving "leaders" of invitation to a visually undetected downward travelling spark, called a "stepped leader"—or vice versa. Uman explains this moment of initiation in terms of speech acts. "What is important to note . . . is that the usual stepped leader starts from the cloud without any 'knowledge' of what buildings or geography are present below. In fact, it is thought . . . that the stepped leader is 'unaware' of objects beneath it until it is some tens of yards from the eventual strike point. When 'awareness' occurs, a travelling spark is initiated from the point to be struck and propagates upward to meet the downward moving stepped leader, completing the path to ground" (1986, 49–50).

We might well ask what language drives this electric conversation that seems to get ahead of itself in the final instant (or was it the first instant?) of divine apprehension—"when awareness takes place"? Uman is certainly uncomfortable about imbuing electricity with human intention, desire, and knowledge, and marks his unease through the use of inverted commas around these attributes, as well as in the frank confession that, "exactly how the stepped leader works is not understood" (1986, 74). But perhaps the difficulties that attend any identification of this fiery first encounter makes more sense if we consider the global canvass of its constant reiteration. Uman explains that "the total current flowing beneath all thunderstorms in progress throughout the world at any given time is thought to be about 2000 amps, and is in such a direction as to charge the earth negatively. An approximately equal and opposite current flows in regions of fine weather. The result is that the net negative charge on the earth and the equal and opposite net positive charge in the atmosphere remain approximately constant" (1986, 153 and 158).

In other words, *one* lightning stroke, moved by a logic that exceeds its binary forces, can also be seen as a stroke in which an entire field of energy rewrites itself; a global field wherein each "particle" is charged by what is seemingly outside and separate from it. Even those tiny molecules of DNA whose different electrical valencies register the banded strings of our body's genetic expression are alive to this moment. In a sense then, a field of electricity is present in the instant, here and yet everywhere, always charging itself by discharging itself, every moment a singular expression that is nevertheless ubiquitously written and read. And if lightning is always/already possessed and entranced by its own disjuncture, little wonder that the origin of its initial desire seems always to escape definitive location.[8]

These examples of an indeterminacy that is nevertheless strangely accurate and finessed in its expression might be understood as instantiations of the graphematic (grammatological) structure, and yet if we do this, then the assumption that language mediates a world that is not always/already language, mediation (of itself), differentiation has no purchase. In sum, my aim here is to interrupt the way that Derrida's *nonconcept* "textuality" or "language in the general sense" has been taken up, knocked into disciplinary shape, properly and predictably contextualized, and, inevitably, conceptualized. If we begin by looking at the consumption pattern of deconstructive criticism within the academy we see a very clear institutional response to the perceived use-value of this "general language." The radical interiority of textuality has been made synonymous with the peculiar and even secret life of signs—with the study of their ubiquity, with their perversely plastic reproductive capacity, their discursive morphologies, and especially with the bipolar gravities that animate their political organization. Although the stretch of deconstructive "textuality" concedes no external perspective, no outside position against which to identify or define what might be unique to the strange vitality of this organism, this articulate enclosure without limits has nevertheless been located and even given a name—*Culture*. The explanatory and productive power of Culture has assumed global proportions as a consequence. Indeed, so powerful are these revelatory and constitutive capacities that they have even unveiled Nature as Culture's creature.

We are surely used to seeing the word "Nature" placed in quotation marks to mark its denaturalization, reminding us that the grounds of perception and evaluation are always/already an implicated context whose representational history uncovers the peculiarities of Culture's investments. However, we should be aware that this corrective remains committed to the logic of origins and causal determination, simply replacing one domain or one notion of initiating efficacy with another—not Nature but "nature," that is, Culture.[9] But what exactly is being managed or claimed in this reversal of constitutive ordering, this maneuver that recovers identity and agency by adjudicating their proper place?

Given the determination that grammatology concerns the workings of Culture proper, there can be little surprise that the economies of scale that might derive from an extension of this reading of "textuality" into disciplines whose objects assume substantial and material solidity in Nature have yet to be robustly explored. However, Derrida has made it abundantly clear that "language in the general sense" exceeds its enclosure within linguistics and its conflation with representational systems as we might conventionally conceive them. If "textuality" does not originate in the atomic unity of the sign, if it is a splitting or trace whose infinite dispersal and genesis confounds all notions of dimensionality as aggregation; place *and* time, cause *and* effect, Culture *plus* its unreadable (and supposedly illiterate) outside (~~Nature~~), then the intricacies of this general writing are not just coextensive with the internal workings of Culture. My point here is not to suggest that we need to "get real" and add Nature's authorship to this strange text, as if Culture's inadequacies might be healed with a natural supplement. Surely, what remains ungraspable even as it enables the questions of "language" and "who writes this text?" to be posed is that the identity and relational purchase of Nature, Culture, and their corollaries, substance and interpretation, are all alive to the same initial conditions that inform the clairvoyance of cellular communication and lightning strokes. In other words, these seemingly separate entities are the *différant* expressions of a unified field, a "general text."

To bring this back to more disciplinary concerns, as the integrity of difference is unhinged from, and yet opened through, the logic of opposition, the difference between the humanities, the social sciences, and even the sciences in regard to their respective objects of inquiry is no longer straightforward and easily defined. Has the question of Nature, or how we might think language and technology in an originary sense, really been posed when we assert that, yes, language is at the "origin" because Culture imaginatively reinvents itself there to replace the irretrievable loss of Nature proper? By assuming that an absolute breach separates Culture, or the intricate structures of agency, information, and its interpretation, from something that preceded it, two autonomous domains are inferred. Culture then absorbs the rupture as its own defining energy and the presumed evolution of this "secondariness" is made synonymous with the birth of human thought and language, and the emergence of complexity and technology.

What is especially disturbing about this way of thinking is not that it reinstates the very logic whose political implications it abhors, namely, equating otherness with an original simplicity and limitedness. After all, such lapses will inhabit every argument to some extent. Yet more serious and difficult to engage is the sense of righteous conviction and benevolent purpose that motors these arguments, rendering them quite incapable of acknowledging the how and why of their resemblance to what they oppose. I am laboring this point because although such insights are prosaic to a critical politics, at least when it applies to an easily identifiable conservatism, there is an unspoken interdiction against discussing the more unpalatable but no less serious and perplexing implications of this lesson's general application.

This elaborated form of Cartesianism where everything is *always/already* a cultural construction foregrounds ideation and the human mind's now enlarged and collective success. However, something is certainly left out of all this, and this "something" leaves us in quite a quandary in regard to the palpable achievements of scientific knowledge. Diagnosing scientific instrumentalism and its political agendas doesn't displace the disarming fact that such knowledges work—sometimes imperfectly, but very often miraculously well. Indeed, it is precisely because they do work, and with such immediate and ongoing physical repercussions, that we bring special scrutiny to these practices and their foundational assumptions. However, there appears to be an operative blind spot here, because instead of encouraging us to rethink our understanding of representation so that it can include such things, for example, as the predictive diagnostics of genetic fingerprinting, the engineering feat of airplane flight, or the spacetime compressions of information technologies, these wonders have been surreptitiously written out of our inquiries. We encourage children to question how the world is put together, delight in their hypotheses, and rely upon science and the arts to complicate and further them. But here is the rub. When it comes to acknowledging how the dimension of scientific capacity might be included in pronouncements about "textual efficacy," the parsimony of much contemporary language sloganeering is sadly in evidence. By assuming that language belongs to Culture so entirely that its complexity is synonymous with it, and by then insisting that a progressivist politics is grounded and guaranteed by this neat equation, the most primary and exhilarating existential questions are significantly circumscribed. Further to this, by adjudging claims about the nature of Nature naive or "precritical," we relieve ourselves of the need to explore the purchase of such truth productions for many of the lived dimensions of contemporary life.

It is as if the fear of opening *the concept* "text" to an outside whose determinations do not begin and end with the human subject is so inconceivable, so seemingly unrepresentable, that it becomes unthinkable; as if the suggestion that the human subject is not the interpretive architect of the world and origin of language simply cannot be entertained.[10] Instead of opening the question of the object *again* (for this is not a simple return to the naiveté of objectivism), science is read as "bad boy" to the humanities' denigrated yet superior sensitivities, a bad boy whose penetrative and instrumental logic must be distinguished from more poetic, creative, and generous curiosities. The "hard object envy" of cultural analysts is denied and yet sadly underlined when political virtue is earned by attributing our world's existential truth to Culture's formal efficaciousness.

I am trying to link several things here that I will briefly summarize before I continue. Discourses such as scientific knowledges that presume to approach or understand an unmediated Nature have been criticized within the humanities because they misrecognize Culture for Nature and mistakenly imbue their subjective interpretations with objective facticity. Cultural analysts make the necessary corrective by insisting that the "initial condition" of the human condition involves a break from the world whose different result is "filled" and repeated by the myriad projections and ideations that language generates. The form versus substance division, magnified as the Culture versus Nature opposition, is intrinsic to this corrective that ironically draws leverage from its refutation: the division is regarded as a problem because it endorses a political economy of inequity that naturalizes difference as base, primordial, and lacking. Given the need for such critical attention, and I am not disputing this, what can we do when the vigilance of our arguments inadvertently reverses and entrenches the very logic that we hope to undermine? Is there something more to "textuality" or "language in the general sense" that might enable a more surprising and provocative outcome; one that keeps alive the counterintuitive and challenging aspects of poststructural criticism rather than dismissing them altogether?

The difficulty in such questions was anticipated at a conference held in 1966 at Johns Hopkins University, where the interdisciplinary possibilities of structuralist and critical theory were fiercely debated. The extraordinary line-up of scholars included such luminaries as Jean Hyppolite, Jacques Lacan, Roland Barthes, Tzvetan Todorov, René Girard, Lucien Goldman, and Jacques Derrida. In the preface to the published conference papers and discussions, the editors note that "the organizers of the program sought to identify certain basic problems and concerns common to every field of study: the status of the subject, the general theory of signs and language systems, the use and abuse of models, homologies and transformations as analytic techniques, synchronic (vs.) diachronic descriptions, the question of 'mediations' between objective and subjective judgments, and the possible relationship between microcosmic and macrocosmic social or symbolic dimensions" (Macksey and Donato 1970, x).

Young and relatively unknown at that time, Derrida presented a paper that constituted a radical assault on the very notion of language and structuration that underpinned the conference thematic. In the round-table discussion that followed Derrida's paper, "Structure, Sign, and Play in the Discourse of the Human Sciences," the distinguished scholar Jean Hyppolite dilated on his own understanding of Derrida's attempt to rewrite the scene of man's genesis by rethinking the ontology of language. As this exchange provides a useful insight into some of the difficulties that Derrida's work announces, it is worth pausing over one of its more provocative moments to try to recapture the energy in this inquiry.

Hyppolite was in agreement with Derrida that the identity of structure was not at all straightforward, and he conceded that the natural sciences have made considerable advances in thinking through its "destructuration." Hyppolite commented:

> I think we have a great deal to learn as we study the sciences of man; we have much to learn from the natural sciences. They are like an image of the problems which we, in turn, put to ourselves. With Einstein, for example, we see the end of a kind of privilege of empiric evidence. And in that connection we see a constant appear, a constant which is a combination of space-time, which does not belong to any of the experiment-

ers who live the experience, but which, in a way, dominates the whole
construct; and this notion of the constant—is this the center? (Hyppolite
in Macksey and Donato 1970, 266)

Hyppolite was interested in this structure that entirely exceeds, indeed, it
even precedes, the structure and vagaries of language as we conventionally
understand them. Musing about this sense of a "before" yet striving to
conserve the motif of language as Derrida seems to do, Hyppolite surmised
that this extension of language into the natural sciences must involve a
form of writing whose origin is dispersed and whose improbable results
"don't come from any author or any hand" (266). Considering the difference between the accomplishment of human language and its primordial
precursor (which ironically enough has "authored" the former) Hyppolite
conceived the break in transmission as a "mutation," likening it to "the poor
reading of a manuscript, realized [only] as a defect of a structure" (266).
This image whereby something primitive generates something intelligent
and immensely complex recalls the image of the proverbial typing monkey.
This is a mathematical reflection about probabilities, sequencing, and infinity that has a monkey hitting the keys of a typewriter at random and for
an infinite amount of time. The suggestion is that the monkey would
"almost surely" produce a great work of literature as part of its massive
output, or, perhaps more accurately, it would not be strictly impossible for
such an outcome to be realized.[11] In a very real sense the great work,
whether literature, or here, the complex language that defines human being
and its capacities, could only arrive as an aberration from the "writing" of
chance sequences and associations. In other words, the human is so thoroughly different that its genesis would be a true "mutation"—an error.

Hyppolite elaborated his position, which he put in the form of a question: "Is it a question of a structure which is in the nature of a genotype
produced by chance from an improbable happening, of a meeting which
involved a series of chemical molecules and which organized them in a
certain way, creating a genotype which will be realized, and whose origin is
lost in a mutation? Is that what you are tending toward? . . . And you know
that the language we are speaking today, *à propos* of language, is spoken
about genotypes, and about information theory" (266). Hyppolite then cut
to the chase. "Can this sign without sense, this perpetual turning back, be
understood in the light of a kind of philosophy of nature in which nature
will not only have realized a mutation, but will have realized a perpetual

mutant: man? That is, a kind of error of transmission or of malformation would have created a being which is always malformed, whose adaptation is a perpetual aberration, and the problem of man would become part of a much larger field" (266–67).

There is certainly something unsettling in the suggestion that Nature, the object that science would decipher, is already a cipher, and one whose errant language games called the human into existence. Language speaks us indeed! However the historicity of *this* language is not synonymous with cultural and social inheritance. We might think that the problem of man as the center of the structure—the sovereign subject—is certainly addressed by this insurrection that would see man dethroned as the origin of language and reader of the world: the harsh reality is that man has become a mutant by-product of Nature's perverse experimental philosophy in Hyppolite's revised history. And yet although Derrida admits sympathy with the direction of Hyppolite's musings he takes "exception" to Hyppolite's "[choice of] words, and here the words are more than mere words, as always. That is to say, I cannot accept your precise formulation, although I am not prepared to offer a precise alternative" (Derrida 1970, 267).

What is there in Hyppolite's "precise formulation" about "the nature and the situation of man *in* the products of nature" (Derrida 1970, 267, my emphasis) that might cause Derrida to pause? At this point in the discussion Derrida seems strangely compelled to question his ability to know quite what he intends to say. Several times he confesses, "I was wondering myself if I know where I am going," and a paragraph later, "I do not know where I am going . . . the words which we are using do not satisfy me" (267). What might be at stake in Derrida's reticence to fully embrace Hyppolite's position seems to concern the philosophers' different understandings of a center, and perhaps more important here, what these different understandings might imply for reconceptualizing linguistic competence and intention within the process (language) of evolution.

To illuminate this difference, we will recall Hyppolite's acknowledgment above that questions in the natural sciences "are like an image of the problems which we, in turn, put to ourselves." Given this, Hyppolite asks Derrida to dilate on the relevance of the Einsteinian constant for the sciences of man.

JACQUES DERRIDA: . . . The Einsteinian constant is not a constant, is not a center. It is the very concept of variability—it is, finally, the

concept of the game. In other words, it is not the concept of some-
thing—of a center starting from which an observer could master the
field—but the very concept of the game which, after all, I was trying to
elaborate.[12]

HYPPOLITE: Is it a constant in the game?

DERRIDA: It is *the* constant of the game . . .

HYPPOLITE: It is the rule of the game.

DERRIDA: It is a rule of the game which does not govern the game; it is a
rule of the game that does not dominate the game. Now, when the rule
of the game is displaced by the game itself we must find something
other than the word *rule.* (Derrida 1970, 267).

As we will see, Derrida's clarification of this riddle seriously contests the
fetishization of language that has become *de rigueur* in so much contemporary cultural analysis. Derrida discusses the difference that a generalized
view of language can make. Taking the example of algebra, a language that
appears to have no grounding center or referent, Derrida explains that "we
can consider algebra from two points of view. . . . [O]ne thinks of algebra as
a field of ideal objects, produced by the activity of what we call a subject, or
man, or history, and thus, we recover the possibility of algebra in the field
of classical thought; or else we consider it as a disquieting mirror of a world
which is algebraic through and through" (1970, 268).

Despite this sense of absolute indetermination and ambiguity Derrida
does not reject the center or the subject, but instead attempts to situate
these "functions" (1970, 271) as precisely as he can. This sense that an
entire field might express itself precisely in/as the subject is evoked in
Derrida's attempt, as we saw above, to explain his intellectual directions by
giving himself up to the game. "I was wondering myself if I know where I
am going. . . . I am trying, *precisely,* to put myself at a point so that I do not
know any longer where I am going" (1970, 267, my emphasis).

We now know that Derrida's way has not been a complacent meander-
ing, or simple loss of direction, but something to which, perhaps, his trust
was already given. Perhaps this sense of opening oneself to a vocational
calling whose intelligent play draws one *expressly,* precisely, animates and
implicates the "awareness" of a lightning stroke, the clairvoyant literacy of
neuronal communication, quantum action at a distance—and all in the
one breath. In my attempt to conjure something of this "awareness" that
drives my own way forward, I've tried to think through the question of

language not as loss of the referent, Nature, the world, but as their playful affirmation. I want to argue that the current wisdom in the humanities that resolves this play by explaining the problematic of language as the reflex of Culture defines language as forfeit and substitution, thus reassigning the center by default. Yet there is an affirmation that "*determines the non-center otherwise than as loss of the center*," that "surrenders itself to *genetic* indetermination, to the *seminal* adventure of the trace," and that "tries to pass beyond man and humanism" (Derrida 1970, 264).

It is to this end that I return to a beginning that tries to think the graphematic structure of human genesis, the scene of its writing, not only as an accidental and mutant afterthought, as Hyppolite's suggestion implies, as if by chance, but also, and necessarily, as a determined forethought whose provocative complexities might be described as "originary humanicity." For there is something in Hyppolite's suggestion that man is a product of the accidental *scribblings* of Nature, accidental because they are authorless and unintended, that places, rather than displaces, the intending and calculating (human) subject *in* this text as an event that arrives, in a narrative, albeit an errant one. How is intention and agency, the self-present and purportedly different arenas of Nature versus the technology of language and human invention, displaced and rerouted if, instead of assuming that we *could* kill the author, or that we could locate the author in a place of only marginal and aberrant importance, we continue to pose the question of the subject, even here, in the implication of the graphematic structure, not just *at* the origin, but *as* originary articulation? What redacted aspects of life's nuanced achievement might reorganize our attentions if originary technicity is conceded its "humanicity"? Does this return us to the purported error and pomposity of anthropomorphic projection, a very subjective and particular view of the world that disavows its actual circumscription, its political prejudice and embodied situation? Admittedly, originary humanicity involves political dimensions that will affirm anthropomorphism, refute anthropomorphism, and entirely redefine what we mean by "anthropomorphism." In other words, this "political physics" will inevitably muddle and reorient our moral compass, unsettling sedimented wisdoms about location, about what constitutes embodiment, and asking why a single perspective might prove more comprehensive and entangled than seems possible.

Importantly, to allow anthropomorphism its non-local ubiquity is not to refuse its specificity, but rather to acknowledge that anthropomorphism's infinite differentiations/specificities are expressions of one phenomenon, one implicated spacetimemattering. How we approach this phenomenon (which includes us), a phenomenon whose identifications entail constant morphogenesis, is to open the question of the human, and writing, as if for the first time.

2. Just Figures?

Forensic Clairvoyance, Mathematics,
and the Language Question

> A written symbol long recognized as operating non-alphabetically—
> even by those deeply and quite unconsciously committed to alphabeti-
> cism—is that of number. . . . But, despite this recognition, there has
> been no sustained attention to mathematical writing even remotely
> matching the enormous outpouring of analysis, philosophizing, and
> deconstructive opening up of what those in the humanities have come
> simply to call "texts."
>
> Why, one might ask, should this be so? Why should the sign system
> long acknowledged as the paradigm of abstract rational thought and the
> without-which-nothing of Western technoscience have been so unex-
> amined, let alone analyzed, theorized, or deconstructed, as a mode of
> writing? (Rotman 1997, 18)

Predictive Mysteries: Giving a Face to the Question

Jetlagged in the déjà-vu routine of hotel arrival and collapse, the mesmer-
ism of my soporific reverie was suddenly interrupted. I think it was a
program on the Learning Channel, one of those forensic journeys of witness. In a way there was nothing especially remarkable about what it had to
say; in fact there are few current prime-time television dramas whose
unfolding plot lines don't refer at some point to similar stories of scientific
sleuthing. On this occasion the narrative focus concerned the discovery of

a human skull, or "anonym" as it is technically called—human remains devoid of any form of identification. Although I don't remember the exact whereabouts of its discovery, I do recall that it was found somewhere in the United States, in the countryside, and that it could have been of ancient or contemporary origin. The dearth of clues maintained the bones' stubborn and seductive mystery, forcing the investigative drama to look elsewhere for answers. But it was the counterintuitive presumption that an entirely different context's data might betray the skull's identity that caught my attention. The investigation assumed, in other words, that things with no apparent connection to the material at hand were somehow integral to its provenance.

Before I discuss the outcome of the forensic artist's endeavors in this particular case I want to make a brief detour to explain the techniques involved in such facial reconstruction. As a preliminary musing in regard to this argument's larger concerns, I also want to consider why fleshing out the contours of soft tissue can elicit such extraordinary fascination. Why do we assume that bone poses a riddle that only flesh can resolve, as if the subject has a dimensional "out-come" or existence on just one surface, as if the face operates as personal signature and guarantee? Perhaps it is the transformed legacy of phrenology, where facial features and their relational arrangements map character and personality traits. For surely we do assume such things. The face arrests us and seems to focus and distill that elusive "something," that individual essence that animates a body's overall demeanor. Similarly, we want to know what people from the past actually looked like because we interpret the face as a register of life's vicissitudes. Although we might be aware of the historical detail that surrounded such figures as King Philip II of Macedon or King Midas, in the recent forensic reconstruction of these men's faces we see a neighbor, a friend, or even an enemy; we look for a familiar resemblance that might provide us with clues to their actual disposition or temperament.[1]

According to the literature, facial reconstructions are a relatively recent undertaking, falling neatly within Michel Foucault's determination of the modern *épistémè* of man's self-interrogation. The first experimental attempts at an accurate identification were undertaken by the anatomist His, who sought to determine if the purported remains of Johann Sebastian Bach were indeed those of the famous composer (Prag and Neave 1997, 15). The relationship of a particular skull to its facial morphology had already been investigated through simple observation, comparing an artist's representation or likeness, such as a portrait bust, with the particular contours of the skull. However, it wasn't until His in 1895 that a scientific method of facial reconstruction was seriously considered. This involved dividing the skull into a template of measurements—a grid of longitude and latitude whose universal intersections provided an anchor for comparison.

Of course, the comparison was no longer between a representational likeness and the bony architecture that might support it, as in the previous example, where ideally one might hope to achieve a match or fit rather than deduce an unknown. The real shift in His's detective work was that it followed a quite alien route of discovery: His began an overall statistical analysis, measuring tissue depths on the faces of cadavers.[2] This undertaking provided a more finessed understanding of facial architecture, as well as the optimistic possibility that from such general measurements a more accurate extrapolation to a specific instance might be possible. A dead person's tissue depths are a little more deflated than in life however, and as these were relatively small samples that took little account of human diversity markers, reconstruction techniques were no more than loose guidelines. More recently, not only has the database for these conjuring acts been radically extended in terms of sample numbers but a diverse range of computing technologies has refined the practice, including ultrasound data from living people, computed tomography (CT scans), and magnetic resonance imaging (fMRIs). The head becomes a sort of global geography in these calculations, where algorithms forecast the skull's cranial grammar in "isosurfaces" that chart the contours of a very individual morphology.

Interestingly, the most common practices in forensic medicine today are still based on the old ones, where an artist working in clay will survey the architecture of the head through pegged, craniometric "landmark sites," twenty-eight to thirty-two points that can each be compared to a statistical archive of tissue depths.[3] In other words, each one of these points involves a differential between the skull's bony proportions and the cephalometric contours of the skin's surface; a variable within a single point. The topography of the head between these sites is then interpolated through the artist's particular feel and experience, working from a knowledge of anatomy built up through the muscles of the face.[4]

A certain amount of information can be derived quite directly from the anonym's skull itself, where the activity of muscle and tendon on the bone leaves evidence of their respective size and strength. The large temporalis muscle, for example, joins each side of the upper skull to an insertion point on the jaw, and the nature of this join gives a significant clue to the muscle's proportion. It is not surprising then that the workings of several local conversations between flesh and bone should be legible to the forensic detective; a straightforward demonstration of cause and effect. Yet even more fascinating is the way that the substance of these local dialogues can be inferred from other places on the skull such that the dimension of their actual locality is strangely disseminated. Indeed, there are aspects to this jigsaw puzzle that completely reconfigure how we might think about coordination, for our notion of association or contact is stretched beyond the common sense of touch in these examples. In other words, although the resonance between separate parts of the skull seems to require no effective proximity, their differences are able to inform and even inhabit each other nevertheless.

Take for example the particularly gruesome case of the "Wyre Street victim." Discovered in 1993 in Manchester, England, this unfortunate person's remains were never meant to be identified, as the decapitated head was discovered with no body nearby. As Prag and Neave describe it, "Due to the severity of the damage all the bone that forms the mid-portion of the face was missing. Thus all the evidence for the shape of the nose, the inner corner of the eyes and the upper lip are absent, and further, the overall integrity of the proportions of the skull were slightly compromised as it was not possible to reassemble properly some of the larger pieces since they had separated along the suture lines" (1997, 38). Yet even here, faceless, and one would have thought forever nameless, calculations from the remaining skull fragments predicted a sufficient resemblance to an Adnan al-Sane, a wealthy Kuwaiti businessman, for someone to recognize him. Thus, a mere fragment of bone may express condensed and diverse information about the skull's lost integrity. These harmonies of the whole within the fragment, where information from one part of the head somehow resonates with another, reappear in larger rendition in the massed tables of statistical death masks and the recent measurements from living subjects that actually "give face" to an anonym. In this general biometry of faciality, what one could regard as a babble of anonymous and general data can nevertheless predictively inform the "landmark sites" with a quite specific contouring signature.

To return to the television program that originally captured my interest, it provided a curious illustration of how a general field of information is condensed, in quite specific ways, *as* an individual morphology. Here again the face of an unknown woman emerged from the numbers, the face of an individual almost *dis*figured by an obtrusively long nose. The forensic artist felt that the nose might even be wrong but decided to simply go with the numbers in the hope that its distinctive proportion, if accurate, might bring a successful identification.[5] And it did. As I recall, of the thirteen people who came forward after the photographic publication in a local newspaper, nine of them were able to give a name to the algorithm's prediction. Follow-up leads discovered the victim's sister, a woman whose resemblance to the clay figure was quite unmistakable and whose intimate kinship was later confirmed with a DNA match.

Although most of us have seen evidence of this same process and its predictive success, we rarely pause to consider how it is possible. Perhaps we are put off by the mathematics involved, assuming that the arcane nature of its apparent prestidigitation says more about our own ignorance than it does about some mysterious puzzle in regard to number. As cultural analysts, even if the actual operations of mathematics exceed our expertise, we might still want to insist that mathematics is a language. But does the notion "language" remain the same when stretched into unfamiliar forms? For example, can we think "signification" *with* "algorithmic prediction," or does the possibility of prediction introduce something that is alien to language?

Given the pivotal importance of language to cultural analysis, the dearth of work that explores how mathematics might "fit" into claims of a "generalized language" is surprising. Brian Rotman, a mathematician with considerable expertise in contemporary cultural analysis and whose question opens this chapter, finds the absence of discussion on this topic a telling one. It seems fair to say that the pragmatic precision of mathematics, evident in the algorithmic predictions of forensic inquiry, sits uneasily with the formulations of language to which we usually refer.

Several points need to be summarized from the above discussion before we move into the next section. First, the forensic scene gives witness to a communicative intimacy, a peculiar correspondence between radically different materials, information, and events. We have seen that data taken from one temporal and spatial location can contain information about another; a fragment of skull is also a sign of the whole, just as an individual skull seems to be a specific expression of a universal faciality. In other words, there is no simple presence versus absence in these examples, no individuated atomic identity that does not, in some way, refer to, or resonate through, a larger context. It is as if the context is somehow within these individual signs, as if they are quantum "entities" that have a specific, delimited locality as well as a global presence or efficacy. Is it possible that these webs of implicated reference might help us to rethink our current understandings of "sign," "textuality," and "language" as such?

Global Geomancies:
"The Most Radical Unity of the World"

In his first book, *Edmund Husserl's Origin of Geometry: An Introduction,* Jacques Derrida explores the ontology of language through the question of mathematics. Derrida notes that "the mathematical object seems to be the privileged example and most permanent thread guiding Husserl's reflection," and the reason for this is that "the mathematical object is *ideal*" (1989, 27). Husserl puzzles over the arrival, endurance, and apparent atemporality of these objects, and we can understand the special weight of his question when we consider that scientific achievement and progress rest on the *effective* deployment of these ideal objects, a point underscored in the title of Husserl's larger project of which the *Origin* was a part—*The Crisis of European Sciences and Transcendental Phenomenology.* Whereas Brian Rotman (1993a, 142) explains the "fit" that mathematics achieves in terms of the contextual location, or corporeal *attachment* of an individual *to* the world (and we will explore this argument more thoroughly in the next chapter), Husserl's meditation puzzles over the logic of supplementarity, that is, the very question of connectivity that attachment assumes without explaining: body *and* language, perception *and* cognition, individual *and* society, subject *and* world, here *and* there, then *and* now. The differences that draw Husserl's special attention, as Rudolf Bernet summarizes them, are "the separation between real (factual) objects and ideal (essential) objects, as well as the separation between external (empirical) history and internal (a priori) historicity" (1989, 141). Although Husserl's argument considers the specific intrigue of a mathematical ontology, it becomes clear that the puzzle of transmissibility, or connectivity, represents an excursion into the question of language more generally.[6]

To unpack this further, Husserl grounds mathematics in perception and experience, that is, in humanity's sensible engagement with its corporeal situation. Geometrical abstraction, he surmises, is derived from the sense perceptions of individual, concrete subjectivity. However, inasmuch as these experiences of the world are necessarily local and personal, a translation of a very particular "being-here-ness," or cultural present, Husserl ponders the intersubjective dimension of their empirical distillation as well as the related question of their historical transmission. Husserl excavates the archaeology of their possibility, wondering how these cultural artifacts of human thought emerge and endure. Although Husserl's question about the language of the sciences addresses the "flowing, vital horizon" (in Derrida 1989, 177) of a very particular disciplinary formation, its relevance to this discussion, as suggested above, has even broader purchase. Indeed, Husserl himself noted his question's generality when he acknowledged that its status was perhaps more exemplary than unique: "What is this, if not the 'theory of knowledge,' [although] in this case specifically the theory of geometrical knowledge?" (in Derrida 1989, 172)

Not surprisingly then, the primal scene wherein Husserl discovers that first geometer, able to perceive and transmit an "ideal" objectivity, or in more recent parlance, a functional representation, is an event whose very possibility and paradoxicality he must extend to "a whole class of spiritual products of the cultural world, to which not only all scientific constructions and the sciences themselves belong but also, for example, the constructions of fine literature" (in Derrida 1989, 160). It seems that the puzzle of ideal objectivities (representations), as Derrida citing Husserl describes it, concerns their " 'continuing to be' and *'persisting factual existence,'* thanks to which they perdure 'even during periods in which the inventor and his fellows are no longer awake to such an exchange or even, more universally, no longer alive.' To be absolutely ideal, the object must still be freed of *every* tie with an actually present subjectivity in general. Therefore, it must perdure 'even when no one has actualized it in evidence' " (1989, 87).

One way of glossing what captivates Husserl's attention is to cast it as the puzzle of Culture proper, a puzzle that inevitably unifies quite specific and apparently discrete behaviors and even cultures as individual instantiations of human thought and expression. The "historicity of ideal objects" fascinates Husserl because it appears to contradict the linearity, causal development, or simple locatability of knowledge acquisition; its inductions and deductions, accumulations and transfers; and thus, both its origin and its *re*-presentation. The finite reality of discovery, with its inevitably idiosyncratic recording, is not Husserl's concern, but rather its essential transmissibility when all that grounds this original perception, this unique event, will be absent. Given this, Husserl asks how the first geometer or proto-scientist could come up with a representation whose "primal establishment" already possessed such intersubjective and supertemporal purchase that it could assume the status of an accurate objectivation. Although a personal invention, this ideal object was much more than a mnemonic marker, a subjective and idiosyncratic symbol invented by and for a lone inquirer's isolated investigations. Derrida summarizes the motivating question that drives Husserl's meditation: "How can the subjective egological evidence of sense become objective and intersubjective? How can it give rise to an ideal and true object, with all the characteristics that we know it to have: omnitemporal validity, universal normativity, intelligibility for *'everyone,'* uprootedness out of all *'here and now'* factuality, and so forth? . . . [H]ow can subjectivity go outside of itself in order to encounter or constitute the object?" (1989, 63).

Husserl's preoccupation with this original act of intellection concerns the enduring identity of the resulting "object," its apparent invariance across the discord of time and even geographical space. For Husserl will grant this "object" such comprehensive and implicit historicity that it will even resonate with/in the enclosures, the hermetic relativities, of quite specific cultural apperceptions (Husserl in Derrida 1989, 175–80). The horizon of this *first* sense then is already replete with the "co-consciousness" of *all* human activity (Husserl in Derrida 1989, 173), an instance of the singular/plural condensation of Everyman and the quantum puzzles of spacetime. Strange geometry. Husserl's argument that the Living Present of a *first* sense is a condensed co-incidence, or virtual communication of *inter*subjective transmissibility, inevitably raises questions about the "instituting origins" of *intra*subjective sense perception. If we think of perception as an assemblage of modalities and timings within the individual, each one registering a different "take" on the world, then how do we explain the lived coherence of a corporeal geometry that can "join the dots" so effectively? As Derrida notes, "Thus, before being the ideality of an identical object for other subjects, sense is this ideality for *other* moments of the same subject" (1989, 86).

   This uncanny structuration seems to anticipate an "intuitional fulfill-ment" in what we normally regard as initial conditions. In other words, it is as if the origin is already alive with what has yet to come, as if it can't be contained as a delimitable moment, separate and distinguishable from others. Importantly, if this is the case then the "reverse" would also be true, namely, that the future isn't so much the unfolding of supplementary moments *in* time, moments whose difference is secured by the distance from an origin now left behind. Rather, the "future" would more accurately reflect the origin's complex identity, its discontinuities or differentiations *with/in itself.*[7] An interesting implication of this ubiquity, this transgres-sion of identity's defining limits, is that we are provoked to ask how the mathematico-geometric problematic that is language is defined against anything. In other words, how is it contained as pure Ideality? Husserl's investigation of origins discovers a structural a priori of diffraction that complicates the presumption that mediation is a "distance between" en-tities of whatever sort. And yet by separating the life world (pure origin?) from the objectivations of scientific language, Husserl contains and limits his argument's generalizability. By parsing the life world in the dative case and freezing its operations, the resulting stasis and stability provide Hus-serl with the primordial grounding for the idea of the Idea. Derrida glosses this part of the philosopher's argument: "As the most universal, the most objectively exhibited element given to us, the earth itself is what furnishes the first matter of every sensible object. Insofar as it is the *exemplary* element (being more naturally objective, more permanent, more solid, more rigid, and so forth, than all other *elements*; and in a broader sense, it comprises them), it is normal that the earth has furnished the ground for the first idealities, then for the first absolutely universal and objective *identities*, those of calculus and geometry" (1989, 81).

   In Husserl's understanding, the precultural foundation of objectivity is severed from the processes that come to interpret it because those pro-cesses constitute the identifying horizon of human existence. Derrida again glosses Husserl's assumptions here: "Whatever *in fact* the first pro-duced or discovered geometrical idealities were, it is *a priori* necessary that they followed from a sort of non-geometry, that they sprang from the soil of pre-geometrical experience. A phenomenology of the experience is pos-sible thanks to a reduction and to an appropriate de-sedimentation" (1989,

50). Thus, abstraction and genesis seem to flow in one direction only, for although the world's "natural present" is given without reserve, or so it seems, its reception by humankind severs exchange with the origin as if "with an ax" (Derrida 1984, 121). Interestingly, this place of the "before which," or "underneath" the interpretive horizon of human intellection, has the peculiar capacity to *unwittingly* produce that horizon from within itself (as well as the creature who stands upon it) as an autonomous and hermetic outcome. Incredible creation.[8] And here we see how the puzzle of genesis is elided when assumptions about production are subsumed within a linear notion of temporality that segregates process from product, the constitu*tive* from the constitu*ted*.

And yet when Husserl disrupts the normal separations that "doing geometry" imply, in other words, when its different component parts (geometer, situation, history, Culture, representation, etc.) begin to collapse together such that every component somehow resonates with another, he radically reconceives the linear/causal logic of genesis as a "this," and *then*, "this." By evoking a sort of global ontogenesis within any "moment" of individuation, whether subjective or cultural, Husserl witnesses a conundrum that the conventional segregation of space from time hides from us. Inevitably, the "how" of identity's emergent *being*, or communicative capacities, is supposedly explained by the proximity or contiguity that linearity underwrites, as if saying that one thing follows another in close succession is sufficient to explain connection, effect, and causality.

Against the tide of this accepted way of thinking, the sustained interrogative energy in Husserl's argument operates as something of a tonic, evoking dimensional condensations *within* linearity. A classical geometry of atomic separation discovers a natural limitation in the horizon of humanity that contains the puzzle of geometry against an outside, a nonhuman. However, rather than dissolve this horizon in order to amalgamate what was previously separate, thereby exchanging exclusion for inclusion, it is the very geometry, or spacing of such binary structures, in this case, the error *and* the corrective, outside *or* inside, that motivates Husserl's meditation. After all, all of these possibilities presume that the line itself is an entity of sorts that occupies, or divides, space. But if space is discontinuous with itself (dividing itself and its divisions), then the self-presence of identity as a circumscribed event, separated from another event, is radically qualified.

The dimensional implications in this last point are difficult and even more provocative than Derrida's clarifying gloss recognizes. Derrida is at pains to problematize Husserl's "common horizon of experience," which "implies that [subjects] can always, immediately or not, stand together before the same natural existent—which we can always strip of the cultural superstructures and categories founded (*fundiert*) on it, and whose unity would always furnish the ultimate arbitration for every *misunderstanding*. Consciousness of confronting the *same* thing, an object perceived as such, is consciousness of a pure and pre-cultural *we*" (1989, 81). Not surprisingly, Derrida's rejoinder here is directed at the reductionist tendency in Husserl's argument that imagines an enduring univocity, or self-presence of the same. Given this concern, Derrida offers a cautionary warning: "But preculturally *pure Nature* is always buried. So, as the ultimate possibility for communication, it is a kind of inaccessible infra-ideal. Can we not say, then, just the opposite of what Husserl said? Are not non-communication and misunderstanding the very horizon of culture and language?" (1989, 81–82)

Clearly, Derrida's aim is to disrupt the possibility of an "absolute translatability" where the world, as Husserl understands it, would be "the universe of objects which is linguistically expressible in its being and its being-such. [Where] men as men, fellow men, world—the world of which men, of which we, always talk and can talk—and, on the other hand, language, are *inseparably* intertwined" (Husserl in Derrida 1989, 162, emphasis added). And as grist for the mill in regard to the essential errancy of language and its uncooperative distillation as a shared "self-same," Derrida reminds us that Husserl's model of language was a very restricted one, limited to "the language of science." Derrida offers a wonderful description of the Joycean exuberance of language in *Ulysses* by way of underlining why Husserl was unable to manage the condensations of poetic language (1989, 82). In its ebullient encryptions, all working together, Joyce's writing clearly threatens the univocity of Husserl's assumptions about objectivation and exactitude. As Derrida comments, "James Joyce [attempted] to repeat and take responsibility for all equivocation itself, utilizing a language that could equalize the greatest possible synchrony with the greatest potential for buried, accumulated, and interwoven intentions within each linguistic atom, each vocable, each word, each simple proposition, in all worldly cultures and their most ingenious forms (mythology, religion, sciences, arts, literature, politics, philosophy, and so forth)" (1989, 102).

Building on this Joycean "thesaurization," Derrida argues that such an endeavor, taken as an exemplary appreciation of linguistic systematicities,

> would try to make the structural unity of all empirical culture appear in the generalized equivocation of a writing that, no longer translating one language into another on the basis of their common cores of sense, circulates throughout all languages at once, accumulates their energies, actualizes their most secret consonances, discloses their furthermost common horizons, cultivates their associative syntheses instead of avoiding them, and rediscovers the poetic value of passivity. In short, rather than put it out of play with quotation marks, rather than "reduce" it, this writing resolutely settles itself *within* the *labyrinthian* field of culture "bound" by its own equivocations, in order to travel through and explore the vastest possible historical distance that is now at all possible. (1989, 102)

Interestingly, Derrida doesn't oppose the equivocity of Joyce's project to the univocity in Husserl's, deciding instead that Husserl's is a "transcendental 'parallel' to Joyce's" (1989, 103). Within the Joycean congestion of language, Derrida finds that an organizing horizon of intelligibility is never abandoned. In other words, something that effectively operates like Ariadne's thread continues to be held fast as Joyce negotiates his way through the linguistic maze. Thus, from a different perspective we see that a will to full comprehension is actually at work here. And for Joyce, the veiled promise of this univocity announces the possibility that, in Stephen Dedalus's words, he might "'awake' from the 'nightmare' of 'history,' . . . [and] master that nightmare in a total and present resumption" (Derrida 1989, 103).

In sum then, Derrida's intervention seems to be directed at the inevitable failure of both projects. Husserl's restricted notion of language is unable to acknowledge its internal vagaries, spectacularly exemplified in the cryptic associations that constitute language, even scientific language. And this suggests that the univocity that Husserl's objectivations require is confounded. On the other hand, Derrida sees no "solution" in the avant-gardism of a Joycean plurivocity, discovering in both positions a will to full and final comprehension that can never be realized. According to this view there is something inherently derelict in interpretation that renders the subject "unfit" to guarantee scientific or even poetic correspondence. But "who" is this subject? And has Derrida identified (and inadvertently closed) the question much too quickly by eliding it with an unexamined notion of the human condition—its unique properties and capacities?

If we think of language as a maze of in-finite differentiation whose fundamental dimensions are still being drawn, then we cannot assume that language is an instrument invented by humankind to access a world from which we are severed. Although we perceive language in the world around us and immerse ourselves in reading it, we may still assume that a radical and defining break separates what we do from what the world does, or indeed, what the world is. Or to put this another way, we don't tend to think of the Joycean or Husserlian enterprise as specific instantiations of an interpretive exercise of global origin. Instead, we commit to the speech/writing split and its segregated entities, assuming that the gift of the world in its pure immediacy is corrupted and imperfectly comprehended by *Homo loquens.* Unfortunately, Derrida's meditation on the question of measurement/language lends itself to such a reading. When the difference of the human is properly identified against the backdrop of the world, with no attention to what writes this identifying outline into existence, we see that the Derridean entanglement of a "general language" is circumscribed: a "general textuality" is not a global articulation *of and by* the world, but rather the restricted and mirrored implications of what the world's substantial absence makes possible for a human author/reader.

Although Derrida's work teaches us to appreciate the fractal labyrinth within any atom of designated identity, its critical purchase is significantly limited if the circumscription of language and the identity of human species being are exempted from this same scrutiny. In other contexts we contest the spatiotemporal coordinates of any identity whose arrival and separation from a "before which" is thought to guarantee its proper place *in* the world. Indeed, Derrida's aphorism "There is no outside of text" helps us to think this relational involvement. If we are unable to enclose this involvement against an outside that purportedly has no language, and if the subject of interpretation is consequently also its object, then we are within the perverse desires of a geomancy, a geo-logy, whose figurations are strangely "fitting." Could the generalized origin of re-presentation, the hiccough of this subject/object shimmering as the "always already not yet," be thought as the Earth's own scientific investigations of itself? If we could entertain the possibility that our questions involve these expanded dimensions, then Joyce's equivocity, intuition, and inexactitude might be read as a virtual filigree of fractal arabesques that unfold *within* objectivation/perception/scientific language. Is there a way to reclaim Husserl's sense of presence and objectivation *in its positivity* by actively embracing the vagaries of poesis as science?

If we think the systematicities of language as a *global* poesis, a "patternment" of energies whose apparent exteriorities must also mark the curious path of an internal investigation, then what we might call a comprehensive form of "self"-alienation is also a will to science (knowledge/re-production/re-presentation). In which case, the proper identity of this global poesis cannot be secured against an outside that is thought to preexist, exceed, or explain it, whether this is the language of science as Husserl assumes, or whether as Derrida implies, it is a common ground that language renders inaccessible, "preculturally *pure Nature* is always buried" (1989, 81).

By making language synonymous with Culture, Derrida locates the birth of language at Nature's grave, thereby removing the living ground that might guarantee perfect transmissibility. However, if encrypt*ing* is the stuff of language as it constantly reconceives its initial conditions, drawing on itself to redesign itself, then this "disinterment" of energies and intensities is not a recovery of something that is dead or absent until the moment of its calling up. A slightly better analogy might be an exhausted endurance athlete who must "dig deep" as she feels her focus and energy waning. She will not call upon energies that she does not already possess. Rather, her task will be to express the energy that she already is, but in a winning way. Thus, to stick with this comparison, there is no radical break in transmission, no radical departure from initial conditions; rather, a different account is being given of that origin, by the origin itself. What emerges from this is considerably more complex than the claim that there is writing *at* the origin, for if there is no departure from "the system," such that the origin is the system's enduring ingenuity, then "the system's" falling out of/with itself *is* the stammer of language.[9]

If we return to Derrida at this point to reconsider his argument we will recall that compensation for the loss of Nature came with the birth of language. Derrida interprets this loss as a limit, or an essential finitude "which we can never radically go beyond" (1989, 82). Clearly, something substantial is presumed to be missing, something we cannot retrieve in order to test the truth of our representations. However, because the nature of this absence is impossible to fathom Derrida argues that "a sound intelligence" will be forced to reinvent the ground of Nature in order to anchor its thematizations. In other words, if our sense of the world is necessarily a second-order construct that we have mistaken for Nature itself, as Derrida seems to suggest, then it follows that there is an operational and constitutive force in language such that "misunderstanding is always a factual horizon" (Derrida 1989, 82). And yet, if we persist in reading Derrida against himself here, and we take his assertion "there is no outside of text" as an invitation to interrogate language rather than to define and assign it differently, then the generalization of language effects a dramatic shift in this scene wherein true or perfect understanding is thwarted by a break in transmission. Instead, what poses as a "radical break" must itself be broken into, broken open, and globally dispersed (written/read) by a process of differentiation whose energies it is.

Importantly, the implication of this reflex does not mark the enclosure of human existence, as if humankind is the author of this scene rather than its peculiar expression. Again, Derrida's representation of this rupture as a fault line that breaks with the origin and thereby proves that Husserl's intuition of the world's "being-present" is mistaken, illustrates the dilemma here. As noted above, Derrida underlines the notion that a foundational misunderstanding must subtend the factual when he comments, "[This] seems all the more true, especially since absolute translatability would be suspended starting the moment the signified could no longer be lead back, either directly or indirectly, to the model of an objective and sensible existent. Every linguistic dimension that would escape this absolute translatability would remain marked by the empirical subjectivity of an individual or society" (1989, 82).

Derrida's aim here is to remind us that for Husserl, "subjectivity is fundamentally ineffable" because it is not caught by science's "direct, univocal, and rigorous language" (Derrida 1989, 82). After all, subjectivity involves a whole range of feeling and apperception that we conventionally explain in terms of individual specificity, and even perfidy. Given this, Derrida concludes that a direct path between signifer and signified is confounded, and that this is even acknowledged by Husserl himself in the philosopher's inability to accommodate the messy entirety of subjectivity within the language of science and objectivation. However, rather than assume that Husserl is defeated in this because a concept cannot anchor itself in *indi-*

vidual perception, as if the atom of an indivisible signifier (perception) really does preexist a signified (concept) that it evokes only to misinterpret, we can take analytical purchase from the Saussurean conundrum that the signifier and the signified are consubstantial. If we do, then the linearity (both temporal and spatial) that Derrida's intervention against self-presence relies upon, with its corollary imputation of atomic separability and causality in one direction, is significantly qualified. Communication is no longer something that is ruined as it moves from one prior event or identity to another that *falls* later, as if by dint of this falling, this break in transmission, an earlier event or meaning must be distorted or misrepresented. If we regard language in the general sense as the system's playing with itself, a sort of masturbatory process where even death is a fecund aspect of life, then language is the world's reproduction of itself through the womb of its own encryption.

Can we entertain the suggestion then, that perhaps the world's "being present" to itself could involve a scene where a geometer surveys a landscape, a geometer who articulates and indeed *is* a specific expression of the world's studied self-absorption? The world's communion with itself would involve giving itself to itself; a *datum* of "presents," blinking in the wonder of its *own* openness and generosity. Importantly, there is no individuate*d* sender in this scene of exuberant unwrapping who is not already in receipt of what has yet to come. For this is not a scene where the spatiotemporal coordinates implied by terms such as "inaccessibility," "unattainability," "excess," "incompletion," "approximation," "the ineffable," "the unrepresentable," and so on, can be anchored by a finitude of enclosed restriction, differentiated from an outside whose timing has yet to come, or whose spacing defies access.

The dimensions of this riddle are perhaps better evoked in the familiar criticisms of phonocentrism. Anyone who has read this far will not be surprised to hear speech described as writing. Put simply, Derrida's interrogation of speech as pure meaning, pure immediacy, its integrity supposedly intact before writing's re-presentation of it, is well known (*Of Grammatology*). However, a certain complacency in the way we grapple with this question is evident when we presume to answer the conundrum by extracting speech from Nature to more accurately locate it in Culture. The reversal of terms from Nature to Culture begins a deconstructive gestalt shift with extraordinary resonances for rethinking the political evaluation and location of an originary *pre*-scription. However, to leave it at that is to make a clarifying category correction that can leave the origin intact, in a place untouched by "writing." By radically displacing the spatio-temporality of "initial conditions," however, as Derrida encourages us to do elsewhere, the question of Nature/the origin can be posed in a way that recuperates and transforms the question's own initial conditions: not just, how might speech be writing, but having considered this and taken on its complexity, *how might writing be speech?* If we refuse this difficulty by explaining the waywardness of the origin in terms of its absence (and Culture's presence), then the issues that Husserl's meditation struggles to explore evaporate, as if their conundrum has finally been answered by putting things in the right place.

Take, for example, the tension in Husserl's work between objectivism and a transcendental thematic. Glossing and elaborating Husserl's argument, Derrida warns:

> Geometry, in effect, is the science of what is absolutely objective—i.e., spatiality—in the objects that the Earth, *our* common place, can indefi-nitely furnish as our common ground with other men. But if an objective science of earthly things is possible, an objective science of the Earth itself, the ground and foundation of these objects, is as radically impossi-ble as that of transcendental subjectivity. The transcendental Earth is not an object and can never become one. And the possibility of a geome-try strictly complements the impossibility of what could be called a *"geo-logy,"* the objective science of the Earth itself. (1989, 83)

Geo-logy, as "the objective science of the Earth itself," is deemed impossi-ble because the reader/scientist's perceptions are grounded by a *particular* earthly location that can only receive, or indeed be, a limited part of the Earth's "relative appearing" (1989, 85). Derrida notes: "The Earth exceeds every body-object as its infinite horizon, for it is never exhausted by the work of objectification that proceeds within it." Immediately after this state-ment he cites Husserl, who draws the same conclusion: "The Earth is a Whole whose parts . . . are bodies, but as a 'Whole' it is not a body" (1989, 85).

This sense of a Whole, internally differentiated into an infinity of frag-ments, is a familiar way of representing a totality. It is, after all, how we commonly understand the workings of any particular language, discrimi-nating it into smaller functional units such as words, letters, or perhaps phonemes. We then posit that the combinatorial possibilities of these elemental arrangements divide the totality of language into particular expressions, much as the Earth's objectivations are described as *fragments* of a geo-logy. According to this distribution, the Whole is the horizon of potentialities that ground the actual combinations or calculations that can be draw *from* it, and in the case of geo-logy, *upon* it. Thus the Whole, or Totality, would exceed its specific instances, and by dint of this exceeding, it follows that a geo-logy of the Earth could not be captured as an objectivation.[10]

However, following Saussure and Derrida, the puzzle of relationality that these thinkers engage is unable to sustain the notion of discrete or locatable units or fragments *in* a system, for the identity of any "unit" does not preexist the system; rather, a "unit" is "thrown up" or "authored" by the system. Importantly (for the complacency of this reading has become routine), the question of relationality isn't resolved, or even complicated, if we query the supposed independence of these units by insisting instead on their dependence and contingency. Relationality is not an "in-between" the *de-tailing* of entities. If the Earth's grammar is necessarily internal, a shifting algorithm, then any "part" of the Earth would be a virtual geometry with hologrammatic resonance rather than a separated entity, broken off from its larger and now absent, or perhaps still attached, totality. Thus, the classical notions of scale and dimension that inform relationality as such are significantly transformed in this calculation. If this virtual "geometry" requires no outside to access the human—for the genesis of humanness would be an internal articulation of and within itself—then, by implication, "the human" would not be bound and restricted by some special lack of access to that same generative unfolding. "The human" would certainly be a unique determination, yet "one" whose cacophonous reverberations would speak of earthly concerns.

Such a scene questions the integrity of human identity as a secondary and more complex outgrowth of something that precedes it—speech/writing, Nature/Culture. Refigured in this *generalized* scene of mathematical investigation, Protagoras's aphorism "Man is the measure of all things" gets more interesting. Instead of reading this as an anthropocentric relativism, or the unique capacity of a creature whose distance from the world defines what we understand as an instrumental objectivity, humankind emerges as an expression of the world's measured subjectivity, a *geo*-metrizing—a *true* geometry. However, inasmuch as this subjectivity is substantially grounded in its own Becoming Itself, this reflexivity could also be styled "the objective science of the Earth itself"—a *geology*. As we saw above, Derrida foreclosed this possibility by defining geometry against geology, as if geometry is a Heisenbergian apparatus whose effects circumscribe measurement in terms of local disturbance. However, if the world itself provides the intention to measure, the object to be measured, and the apparatus through which that calculation will be determined—why is this not a geology, an earthly science?

Face Value: Giving a Different Account

Finally, we can return to the scene of forensic discovery that opened this meditation and consider the evidence whose rebus uncovers literature inside mathematics and geometry. And more than this. The figure of the face would appear to incorporate a connective tissue wherein flesh and bone resonate with numbers and names; figures, figurations, *la figure*. There is surely something decidedly uncanny about this infrastructural conversation, or is it a conversion, for the particular face whose identifying coherence has yet to be discovered is mirrored in other faces that reference its particular coordinating contours. But how is the unique face of an anonym evident in the myriad faces that have never encountered it? What countenance is this whose likeness is found in the anonymity of statistical tables, shards of bone, the electromagnetic bands of DNA signatures, or the scan's tomographic separations? Identity in this instance isn't secured *against* a ground of scattered and diverse evidence. It is not a delimited "something," an individual thing, confined only to a particular place and time, substance, or form, for it arises in reflection and refraction. This strange unity, at once dispersed and yet coherent, is alive in such notions as "the field," "system," and "structure," terms whose intricate and mysterious dimensions Jacques Derrida attempts to acknowledge as "textuality" or "language in the general sense" in other contexts. As he notes, "*Différance* is a reference and vice versa" (1988, 137).

Whatever language is—organizing tool or instrument, articulating technology, organism—it commands dominant status in the definition and explanation of humanity's species privilege. Made synonymous with sociality, abstraction, and therefore intellection, human language becomes an exemplar of species smarts, a standard against which our difference from the great apes, for example, is secured. Their comparatively puny vocabulary in "natural languages" becomes proof of an intellectual proximity and yet failure, a failure that *Homo loquens* demands. However, if language marks *the* anthropological break, then how do we explain pheromonal literacy in ants, to take an obvious example, or even their adaptive resourcefulness, given that we are likely to account for their superorganismic creativity in terms of a hard-wired, instinctual "pro-*gram.*" What is a pro-gram or instinct that it can accommodate and reinvent itself in terms of external and unexpected exigencies? A reading/writing program? Or perhaps we might consider the viral and bacterial calculating technologies whose cryptographic speed and inventive capacities explain the increasing ineffectiveness of antibiotics? How should we understand epistemology in such an instance where calculation *is* an ontologizing process of mutation? And how can the complexity of genetic grammar be so comprehensively structured that the cold tolerance of flounder can find a home in the alien codes of the tomato plant? Although opponents of genetic engineering invariably argue that these "things" would never have intercourse but for the perverse desires of human experimental voyeurism, my point here is that their interpretive intercourse or ontological confusion has already been anticipated such that a translation is even possible.

These few examples suggest that the language of life is an in-formational bio-logy whose involvements have little respect for species division, even though they produce them. Further to this, our notion of language is extended and complicated if we concede that the infrastructural components of a *bio*-logy are an implicated *geo*-logy, thus confounding the simple difference between living systems and inert, physical matter, or between information and the body that bears it.[11] By opening the question of language, or the geometry of relationality and the partitioning and agglomerative iterations of mathematics to a general and generative field of expressivity, it is not at all clear how we would exclude the poetry of molecular parsings whose alphabet is the periodic table—chemical vocatives for assemblage and dissociation. A metaphor of language? Or more instantiations of a language whose "langue" involves the Earth itself? What subject speaks these messages? Who authors and reads them? How, or why, should we censor these questions from their *natural* extension? For if humanity is not the origin of re-presentation, if the Earth re-presents itself to itself, then repetition must be domiciled with/in Presence.

In retrospect, it is perhaps unsurprising that my attentions were held by the example of forensic revelation because, although it was fascinating in itself, I was already familiar with this puzzle of wild, informatic madness. I can remember how my interest was pricked when I first read about *la folie de Saussure*, his obsession with anagrams. And I was especially touched when I learned that his success in analyzing language into an apparently infinite regress of decomposing units, or "discursive" subensembles, led him to the conviction that perhaps he was witnessing his own mental disintegration rather than an actual operation within language. The problem of the anagrams would later be conceded in a much more manageable form in Saussure's description of the associative axis of language, where the linguist tried to evoke its shimmering activity in a phrase that has always enchanted me—"units living underneath the word" (Saussure quoted in Gadet 1989, 85). For one has a definite sense that this is some strange expression of life, these energy flows of "words upon words." Saussure believed that the anagrams (or were they hypograms, antigrams, paragrams, paramorphs, paramimes, or paratexts) that seemed unaccountably hidden in Latin verse were evidence of authorial intention, examples of poetic conventions that had been lost to history. He was sufficiently perplexed by these cryptic messages to seek proof, as he put it, that they were "deliberately and consciously applied" (Starobinski 1979, 118). But as Saussure's cryptographic skills developed he was soon discovering a stream of anagrams everywhere he looked, even in the most banal of prose fragments. As Sylvère Lotringer describes it, the linguist was clearly troubled by "the sight of [these] words offering themselves up *without his having looked for them*, outside of the individual motivation in which he strictly intend[ed] to contain them" (1973, 8). Indeed, he was presented with such a saturation of possibilities, a veritable "quagmire" as Jean Starobinski describes it, that he commented, "One reaches the point of wondering whether all possible words could not actually be found in every text" (Saussure quoted in Lotringer 1973, 8).

What needs to be remembered here is that Saussure's alchemy, his ability to evoke names as if from nowhere, from the patterns within letters, the spacings, aggregations, repetitions, mirrorings, and so on, discovers within what he hoped was "the proper object of linguistics" the improper calculations of mathematics. Lotringer reminds us that the linguist's focused entry into the anagrammatical spirit of the letter discovers "an *algebra* of discourse" that "define[s] a domain which can no longer serve as an anchor-point for Western metaphysics: pairings, 'regular balancing by numbers,' formulas, itemizations, remainders—the space of the number: 'The ideal poetic line would be one offering, for example, a total: 2 L's, 2 P's, 4 R's (=2+2), 6 A's, 6 O's, 4 U's, and so forth' " (Saussure in Lotringer 1973, 3).

This system of nonlinear, extratemporal correspondences, a counter-discourse of apparent disconnection, abandons the referential guarantee of sign and meaning. It acknowledges a "play" whose lineage has no pre-text or prior phoneme to anchor the intentional direction of its original motivation/author through linearity/causality. Lotringer makes an interesting point in this regard, disputing the interpretive gloss and resolution offered by André Leroi-Gourhan that "number, in effect, is . . . simply the 'historical' instrument of the word" (1973, 3). Drawing on Derrida's argument in *Of Grammatology*, Lotringer notes that "making the number reappear in language reactivates the subversive function that mathematical notation, like oriental writing, has continually brought to bear upon the ideology of the alphabet" (1973, 3–4). Nevertheless, it is clear that coherence is recuperated in Saussure's attempt to return to the name: "The name (*nom*) is only the shadow (*ombre*) of the number (*nombre*). . . . Saussure, naming the number, calling (*appeler*) it names, will have to be content with spelling it out (*épeler*) through the text, citing it element by element, under the umbrella of the Sum which, from then on, only remains to be recited" (Lotringer 1973, 5). Saussure's struggle to repair the travesty of the name's disfigurement is evident in his hope that "the great gain will be knowing the starting point of the anagram" (quoted in Starobinski 1979, 93). However, he did concede that the phenomenon might prove a retrospective illusion projected there by the reader, and one can only surmise that he came to this conclusion when he abandoned the project.

However, today, and without the burden of Saussure's mental anguish and personal misgivings, we might presume that we can answer Starobinski's question, "Was Saussure mistaken? Did he allow himself to be fascinated by a mirage? Do his anagrams resemble the faces one can read in ink-blots?" (1979, 122). Can our answer, even if its status is appropriately qualified by an envelope of inverted commas, actually do justice to the figure's insistent appearance, not simply in an ink blot or in the garrulous underwriting of poetry and prose, but also in the anagrammatological[12] babble that delivers itself to the forensic artist as a face, and more often than not, as a name? The sobering question is how an informational chaos whose poetics exceed even the wildest Joycean associations, can neverthe-less cohere with such "unreasonable effectiveness."

To recapitulate the riddle, Saussure had clear evidence of an operation within language whose "motivation" is not simply linear and whose man-ifestations were strangely phantasmatic. The vagaries of this operation's temporal spacing involved a vertigo of infinite connections and disjunctions whose associative involvements were utterly improper and impossibly per-verse. They certainly weren't obedient to the pragmatic categorizations of linguistics, and yet they appeared to be obedient to something. As we know, Saussure was unable to contain and describe the anagrammatic phenome-non, and he consequently failed to preserve the unity of the sign or word in substitute form by giving face to this operation, this "motivation," in a particular author's intention. Lotringer argues that Saussure's need for a grounding explanation was felt as a crisis, forcing him to "surround himself with guarantees and to exorcise coincidences, according to a neurotic pro-tocol. . . . A completely different conclusion might have imposed itself: not a panicky reclaiming of the whole, but a presentment of the productive func-tion that devolves on any reading as soon as it escapes from the constraints of linearity and the snares of meaning. The recognition of other modes of significance alien to the subject-sign matrix could then be reached, and the semiotics freed from the tyranny of speech" (1973, 8).

This reading is surely well known, this defacement, this decomposition of a subject whom Lotringer describes as "the master of the name and the receptacle of meaning" (1973, 5). Lotringer's diagnosis of "the linguist's incapacity to fracture the enclosure of the subject" (1973, 6) rests on in-sights from psychoanalysis that disperse authorial intention as well as the self-presence of meaning. Humanism is certainly rattled to the core as pretensions to self-knowledge founder. But does Lotringer's gamble with "the game of the name" risk anything more than the (human) subject's *internal* coherence? In other words, is the identity of human species being, its separation and difference from what is purportedly not human, also brought into question through the destabilization of this game?

Lotringer explains the foolishness of Saussure's search for the presence of meaning and intention in terms of the failure of reference and the absence of speech. And in this, we see how Lotringer has assumed that language is a technology unique to *human* subjectivity, a technology whose creation and puzzle defines the human condition, secures its identity, and separates its inventive complexity from an enduring world of substance and stability. Although Lotringer criticizes Saussure's "panicky reclaiming of the whole," from a different perspective Lotringer also suffers from "the linguist's incapacity to fracture the enclosure of the subject" (1973, 6), as well as Saussure's inability to relinquish "the master of the name and the receptacle of meaning" (1973, 5). Lotringer perceives that language is its own receptacle, grounding itself in its own self-reference. However, the need for a unified referent, an absolute and stable ground that is *not* subject to this algebra, means that Lotringer must locate the motivational resonance and complexity of language within the enclosure of a specifically *human* capacity. However, my purpose here is not to simply go another round, nay-saying Lotringer, nay-saying Saussure, for there is something important in both positions that a negative critique forecloses.

First, I have always regarded Saussure's struggle to determine the proper object of linguistics as an insightful exercise or documentation of the ontology of language. Saussure abandons the referent (by way of his critique of nomenclature) only to recuperate it. He segments the sign into its constitutive parts only to then confuse the terms and confound their difference. He elides reality and language in the very gesture that is meant to prove their absolute separation. He also insists that there is nothing arbitrary about language because convention, or historicity, forge a systemic necessity, and yet he is perhaps best known for claiming "the arbitrary nature of the sign." He insists that language follows orders, linear protocols, and yet his work on glossolalia and the anagrams subverts linearity and complicates the notion of *valeur* as equivalence. And throughout his work, significant predictions about the elementary data of linguistics emerged in mathematical calculation, thereby confusing the respective integrity of both "systems." No wonder Saussure was troubled!

Saussure's problem was that while he wanted to acknowledge a motivational coherence whose systemic implications conjured some working sense of a referent for a language community, he also wanted to concede that the identity of any datum was inherently plastic. However, if he understood that language involved a sort of living mutation *within* stability (indeed, this is what he meant by "system"), he struggled to conceive how he might be investigating the workings of a general operation, a "semiology" as he called it, rather than something peculiar to linguistics. The broadening of this operation is perceived by Lotringer when he implicates the subject's psychology, memory, and lived experience in the algebra of language, thereby fracturing the subject's sense of self-certainty and conscious accountability. However, Lotringer contains the extent of the rift when he makes language synonymous with humanity, thus guaranteeing the certainty of identity in the very gesture that questions it. With language as the ideational substitute and compensation for the loss of the world (*Mother* Nature, the pure plenitude whose umbilical connection is severed), the enclosure of language becomes totalizing and perception is inevitably deemed a *mis*recognition. Given the critical importance of psychoanalysis, it is not surprising that Derrida's "no outside of text" has been enlisted into such a reading, despite the philosopher's criticism of the misplaced nostalgia that posits an originary "before" whose presence has been lost to language.

In psychoanalysis, language/writing is thought to displace a referent/reality that is no longer present, and indeed, it is this "splitting off" from reality that forms the constitutive bar that enables language to stand in as reality's representational substitute: by separating the signifier from the signified, the bar prohibits any final coherence that might come from their merger even as it fuels the animating desire to fix meaning once and for all. Against this reading, Derrida's complication of language invites us to begin, not with a loss of the origin that textuality replaces, but with an original (worldly) writing through whose radical interiority the referent *presents* itself. Although it is conventional within deconstruction to claim that the referent, or indeed, any identity, is deferred or displaced, and to understand this to mean that the "entity" we strive to grasp has eluded us and exceeded representation, a more rigorous reading of an originary systemics would complicate this conclusion.

If we place "the human" under erasure in much the same way as we do "language," such that the subject in question is now "language itself," then how can language fail to adequately re-present itself if re-presentation is what language is/does?[13] If difference is not a simple substitution of one thing for another, or a space *between* (self-present) entities, then within the constancy of "the whole's" internal differential there could be no failure to "measure up." Given this reading, "presence" and "speech" no longer provide an origin whose absence allows "writing" and "Culture" to comfortably define themselves, for the immediacy and "presentment" of speech expresses the energetics of an originary unfolding—a writing. Is it possible that the calculation of the subject might be written so expansively, chaotically, and yet concisely, that there is no failure of reference, for the world gives it countenance?

Returning to the vocational calculations of flesh and bone that hail a name through forensic calculations, we should remember that in these instances a name is given, and heard, by a "cast" of thousands, as if by chance. Although it includes the living and the dead, and even, in principle, the faces of those who have yet to be born, there is a strange precision in the dense weave of its allusion (*alludere*—the joke or play of referral). Saussure's sense of "units living underneath the word," or his apprehension that "all possible words could . . . actually be found in every text" is suggestive of this orienting congestion. We are also reminded here of Husserl's puzzle over the "flowing vital horizon" that animated any apparent instance of measurement and representation. If we complicate Saussure's comments here by way of Jacques Derrida's "generalized writing" or "textuality," then the archive of the world, or more accurately, an archive of world-ing, would present itself in every word, underwriting the flesh of every name—every calculation.

These are difficult thoughts that harken back to concerns in the previous discussion about the nature of mathematics, or the calculations of Nature. Derrida helps us here with an early comment from his discussion of Jean-Jacques Rousseau, a comment that sees him also trying to acknowledge the generous dimensions of language and its unqualified dispersal/condensations:

> There is nothing outside of the text [there is no outside-text; *il n'y a pas de hors-texte*). And that is neither because Jean-Jacques' life, or the existence of Mamma or Thérèse *themselves*, is not of prime interest to us, nor because we have access to their so-called "real" existence only in the text and we have neither any means of altering this, nor any right to neglect this limitation. All reasons of this type would already be sufficient, to be sure, but there are more radical reasons. . . . [I]n what one calls the real life of these existences "of flesh and bone," beyond and behind what one believes can be circumscribed as Rousseau's text, there has never been anything but writing. (1984, 158–59)

Within this expanded and more intricate sense of textuality we can see that Lotringer's attempt to undo "the enclosure of the subject" never really questioned the integrity of the subject's outline. It was always a *human* subject whose interiority was to be complicated because, after all, "the human" defines complication against a background that lacks it. Thus, a nonhuman and inarticulate outside was always assumed, an outside that was not subject-ed to/through the game of naming and its astonishing presentiments. In other words, the question of the subject is here *naturally* circumscribed, and the phrase that Lotringer uses to encapsulate self-presence, "the tyranny of speech," is recuperated in the assumption that speaking, or language, properly belongs to human identity—the tyranny of the human.

This representation might be judged unfair, for it is not so hard to acknowledge that Nature, safely contained within inverted commas of course, may well babble. But surely the point here is that we assume that this babble is, indeed, babble—and that it could never manifest the discursive subensembles of the anagrams, assume the subtle patterns of cryptography, read a name, or recognize a face. For even if we grant the term "language" to Nature in its vaguest capacities and remark on the invention of its programs, we will probably assume that such "systematics" are not part of a general conversation that would incorporate, and actually *be*, what we are used to describing as "cultural constructions."

If we take very seriously the notion of an originary writing/*mathesis*, then intelligence, agency, literacy, and numeracy are implicated in the ontogenesis of scriptibility. And with no *pre*-scription, no natural exemption from writing/technology/invention, then the question of language (and being, more generally) radically presents itself. We are used to containing the contagion of language within the human repository, and this management strategy is shared by both humanism and antihumanism alike. Even feminism and minority discourses that maintain critical vigilance in regard to property rights and borders argue against their inclusion in Nature (and consequent exclusion from Culture proper). However, if the default line of political and ethical strategies rests on questioning the distinction between Nature and Culture only to reinstall the division with greater accuracy, then the divisiveness and oppositional violence that this ax cut wields must return to lacerate us in ways we will refuse to own. The interrogative energies of antihumanism, which contest prescriptive identities and behaviors, explain mutation and possibility in terms of the constitutive forces in *Culture.* However, a more radical commitment to a horizon of possibility and change that embraces this dictum *without reservation* might argue that "there is no outside of Nature." What do we forfeit in claiming Nature's "textuality," its literacy, as our own?

3. Enumerating Language

"The Unreasonable Effectiveness of Mathematics"

Evidence of the predictive success of forensic investigation is now pivotal to the narrative disclosure of many television drama series and scientific documentaries. We are used to seeing criminal profilers and laboratory sleuths sift through abject detritus each night on our television screens, looking for patterns of connection and causality. Increasingly, we come to expect that the cryptogram of the crime scene is a riddle that will be solved. Yet as a layperson with no specialist expertise to provide an explanation, the simple question "How is this possible?" remains compelling. Of course, the question is simply answered by acknowledging the algorithmic predictors and other forms of mathematical computation that translate between the seemingly random and the structured, the possible and the probable, the material and the abstract.[1] However, the "transubstantiation" or magical alchemy that allows mathematics to render different materials into completely foreign forms and values must surely make us ponder the ontology of mathematics itself.

Interestingly, mathematics is rarely included in contemporary analysis about Culture and representation because to discuss mathematics implies that you can *do* mathematics. As a result, many of us quietly leave the field to its own practitioners. We surmise that the arcane nature of mathematics and its powers of prestidigitation reveal more about our own ignorance than they do about some mysterious puzzle in regard to number. With good reason we imagine that for many mathematicians there is no mystery, just a series of problems to be solved by an economy of logic whose provocations are easily explained. However, as one writer on the subject, Keith Devlin, describes it, mathematics in essence is *"the science of order, patterns, structure, and logical relationships"* (2000, 73). In his primer on mathematics provocatively titled *The Maths Gene*, Devlin argues that mathematics is a language like any other, with an internal algorithm of combinatorial possibilities.

A system of relational configurations that refers to itself, mathematics would appear to satisfy the linguist Ferdinand de Saussure's most basic perceptions about language. Mathematics also replicates the difficulty one finds in identifying the essential unit, or "object," that explains the system's functionality. And yet even for those of us familiar with the Saussurean legacy and its implicit challenge to what we conventionally mean when we say "language," the connection between the lean reductions of calculation and a natural language such as English feels strained. The most cursory consideration might posit that the ludic quality of natural languages involves a surfeit of figural possibilities, an exuberance of meanings and emotional registers that outstrip comparison. And surely, this wealth of expression seems so dimensionally intricate, inventive, and comprehensive that it authorizes the special place conceded to language in contemporary criticism, and more powerfully, the special place assumed by that species whose privilege it explains—*Homo loquens.*

We have an intuitive sense that the nature of words and how they operate are entirely different from how mathematics functions. The productive imprecision of words, for example, as well as the subjective nature of interpretation, seem quite contrary to the definitional ratio and exactitude of mathematical thinking. What exactly are mathematical symbols about? What is a mathematical object? Is mathematics a language, a cultural invention, or something whose very exactitude and general applicability authorize more universal and objective pretensions? And if it isn't the latter, then how does it work as if it is? Or, if mathematics is a language that refers only to itself, then how can it be so globally inclusive? How can it resonate with biological and chemical information, anticipate the discovery of distant suns and planets, assist in the deciphering of foreign and encrypted literatures, and inspire musicians to express themselves in new forms?

Brian Rotman, a mathematician and cultural analyst, ponders the semiological specificity of mathematical notation. Happily, Rotman's ability to make the disciplinary crossover intelligible to the uninitiated provides an effective toe hold that can "open up mathematical writing in a direction familiar to those in the humanities" (1997, 28).[2] There are very good reasons, however, other than disciplinary ignorance, that make it hard to think mathematics through the general inflation of the term "language," or at least, through the familiar horizon of the term's current deployment in cultural criticism. Quite obviously, the peculiar efficacy in mathematics must be admitted, and yet this concession seems to return us to a battery of terms whose prescriptive truths the term "language" is meant to betray. The assumption that mathematics is the language of Nature, or that its representational veracity evidences the guidance of divine authorship, appears throughout history and is even today held by many practitioners. It is the basis of the perception that mathematics is discovered rather than invented, and its endurance suggests that it is not easily countered. Rotman provides a helpful summation of the problem:

> Why should the timeless truths discovered by mathematicians pursuing their own exclusively abstract, internally motivated, and nonempirical interests provide such an apt description of the empirical world? What *is* the cause and the source of the "unreasonable effectiveness of mathematics"? What indeed? Short of invoking a deity (the source of the miraculous "gift") responsible for the creation of both mathematics and the world—essentially the response of Galileo, Newton, Leibniz, and many after them—what could provide the basis for the "profound mathematical harmony of Nature," as the physicist Roger Penrose recently put it? (1997, 140)

The different ways in which the mystery of this question is comprehended illustrate an increasing antagonism between the sciences and the humanities: it has seen the development of research communities whose respective commitments and specialist languages can be so different that productive dialogue between them becomes strained. C. P. Snow lamented the development of these "two cultures" in the 1950s, and the more recent Sokal hoax, together with the sheer pace and demand for scientific innovation and the difficulty of critically digesting it, has exacerbated the problem.[3]

In acknowledgment of the current situation my aim is to consider how those of us on the humanities' side of the divide might facilitate the possibility of future dialogue with the sciences, for if we are to continue to diagnose and critique certain scientific assumptions and methodologies, then it seems only fair to apply similar scrutiny to our own analytical tools. Cultural analysts have certainly privileged the productive efficacy of language and representation, indeed, even to the extent that "language" absorbs whatever it is defined against. But can the term convincingly accommodate scientific observation, and are we sufficiently persuaded by our claims that we can justify them in rigorous detail? In short, can we be satisfied that by replacing Nature with Culture as the origin, or delimited "system" of productive implication, we can adequately explain "the unreasonable effectiveness of mathematics?"

In "Thinking Dia-Grams: Mathematics, Writing, and Virtual Reality," Rotman takes up the language question by addressing the assumption within scientific thinking that mathematical rigor derives from a "foundational hygiene," a universal truth that predates its inscription. Arguing against this, Rotman reminds us that in a very real sense "rigor" is just another name for the dictates of scriptibility. It is "an intrinsic and inescapable demand proceeding from writing: it lies within the rules, conventions, dictates, protocols, and such that control mathematical imagination and transform mathematical intuition into an intersubjective writing/thinking practice" (1997, 28).

As we saw above, Devlin also insisted that mathematics is a language. However, by lingering over the assertion with particular regard to the status of mathematics as writing, Rotman alerts us to an inattention in our notion of "writing," and indeed, in our easy convictions about what constitutes "language itself." Although Rotman's argument contests the production of a purportedly pure mathematical writing, it is his argument's more general implications that are especially interesting and to which the following discussion will eventually return.

Rotman maintains that contemporary conceptions of language tend to reduce the diversity of symbolic systems and their specificities to "the alphabetic dogma" (1997, 25), where writing is taken as a second-order invention, parasitically dependent on a prior articulation that explains it, such as speech. According to this view, speaking is granted an original fullness, an in-the-world referential life and immediacy that writing, a second-order counterfeit, can only copy and inevitably corrupt. Of course, this line of theoretical criticism that exposes the political implications in this conceptual two-step has cut a well-worn path, as Rotman acknowledges.[4] And yet despite the importance of these arguments their general insights are rarely brought to signifying practices other than alphabetic notation.

Rotman offers a shorthand description of the mathematical community's current convictions about the nature of its objects. "Platonism is the contemporary orthodoxy. In its standard version it holds that mathematical objects are mentally apprehensible and yet owe nothing to human culture; they exist, are real, objective, and 'out there', yet are without material, empirical, embodied, or sensory dimension" (1997, 18).[5]

According to Platonic realism, mathematical signs can have no constitutive relevance, a conclusion that Rotman considers a "travesty" because it quietly erases the material context and bodily engagements that make semiosis possible. Dismissing the *question* of representational veracity, as if performative achievement is a de facto form of explanation, also "mak[es] an enigma out of mathematics' usefulness" (1997, 18). Thus, for Platonists, there is a clear distinction between numerals and number. Mathematical writing, with its diverse historical and cultural representations, is perceived as "a neutral and inert medium for describing a given prior reality—such as that of number—to which it is essentially and irremediably posterior" (1997, 19). But how is the actual process of doing mathematics eliminated, and why should this exclusion, presumed or achieved, be desirable?

As we will see, trying to think through this question is deceptively complicated, even, or perhaps especially, for those whose training in the humanities has provided the question of "writing" with a well-rehearsed response. For something odd begins to happen when our concept of writing shifts from literature to mathematics, something that seriously compromises the apparent autonomy and identity of these different systems of representation, and more importantly, what we are used to saying about them. Rotman leads us into this unavoidable mire by explaining that the actual stuff of mathematical writing is effectively "invisibilized" through a transposition with the conventional linear morphology of alphabetic writing. He notes that, "within the Platonist program, this alphabetic prejudice is given a literal manifestation: linear strings of symbols in the form of normalized sequences of variables and logical connectives drawn from a short, preset list determine the resting place for mathematical language in its purest, most rigorously grounded form" (1997, 26).

Thus, strings of ideograms that appear in an unfolding line of calculation also operate to code this linearity as logical and indeed, as properly mathematical. As Rotman explains, "There are ideograms, such as '+,' 'x,' '1,' '2,' '3,' '=,' '>,' ' . . . ,' 'sinz,' 'logz,' and so on, whose introduction and interaction are controlled by rigorously specified rules and syntactic conventions" (1997, 25). Diagrams, however, those "familiar lines, axes, points, circles, and triangles, as well as all manner of figures, markers, graphs, charts, commuting circuits, and iconically intended shapes," become superfluous to this linear expression of mathematics proper (1997, 25–26).[6] The peripheral status accorded these particular inscriptions is clear evidence of their compromised value as "figures." Read against the unfolding sentence structure of a normative mathematical logic then, these diagrams become figur*al* ornaments or superfluous illustrations. Rotman notes that "however useful and apparently essential for the actual doing of mathematics, [diagrams] are nonetheless merely figurative and eliminable. . . . [M]athematics, in its proper rigorous formulation, has no need of them" (1997, 26).

If the accommodation of figures inside a horizontal typographic line defines the rational grounding of the discipline, it follows that drawing outside the line will appear as an attenuation of this defining protocol, something "metaphorically unrigorous" (1997, 26) and comparatively imprecise. But why should one form of writing become *the* logicosyntactical convention of mathematical discipline, especially when at the same time there is an accompanying deemphasis of its actual manifestation as writing? Rotman suggests that alphabeticism's installation of the gram's implicit and prior sayability is at work here: "One cannot, after all, *say* a triangle" (1997, 32). But this is too swift, and it moves over a hidden complexity in the speech/writing couple that Derrida's work has been at pains to explore. Derrida argues that "linearism is undoubtedly inseparable from phonologism" (1984, 72). However, the point he is making is not explained by the script's actual sayability or otherwise. Rather, his attention is focused on "the concept of time that guides this affirmation and analysis: time conceived as linear successivity, as 'consecutivity' " (1984, 72).

Phonologism imbues certain entities and events with a temporal priority and therefore an ontological integrity that must be diluted or changed from the outside, in this case by *later* circumstance. Derrida's intervention questions the autonomy of identity, arguing instead that what appears as a discrete and delimited particularity, identity, or event is actually an entanglement of systemic energies ("writing in the general sense"). In other words (and this is very much my gloss), any "unit" is not so much a separate part of a larger whole to which it remains indebted, but rather a unique instantiation of the system's own reinvention (or rewriting) of itself. Thus, every "instance" *is* "the whole," and this imploded, holographic sense of identity confounds linearity as an unfolding sequence of separate, successive moments. To return to Rotman on the issue of linearity in light of this, although he does explain phonologism elsewhere in terms of the problems of secondarity (1997, 26), it remains unclear why he assumes that "one cannot, after all, *say* a triangle." The implications of Derrida's argument would encourage us to ask "why not?" What, after all, is speaking that it is not an inherent animation with/in any mark? Or to put this in a different way, we might consider why the sayability of alphabetic notation is any less problematic for those figures than for any others.

Despite the qualifications in these queries, the effect of the specific discrimination that Rotman describes suggests that a speech/writing split does operate *within* mathematical representation, a discrimination that works to disguise the fact that mathematical language, even in what is considered its essential and "proper" expression, is always a writing practice. However, the success of this disavowal, coupled with the confusion in Rotman's corrective about what constitutes sayability, suggests that the very terms of the debate and the positions they anchor are quite slippery. Given this, is Rotman's lapse simply repaired, or is it symptomatic of something in the speech/writing divide that might actually change the very terms at issue?

As suggested above, mathematics circumscribes its illustrative logic in the standard form of a sentence and "the timeless and agentless language of sets" (Rotman 1997, 20). This formal structure then operates as the axiom of mathematical rigor, or "what is cognitively and aesthetically attractive about mathematical practice . . . the source of its utility and transcultural stability" (Rotman 1997, 22). Interestingly, however, the conventional direction of the speech/writing split is reversed in this instance. To explain this, we will recall that the voice is regarded as the true, corporeal expression of lived experience and the realization of personal intention. It is as if the voice captures, or more profoundly, the voice *is*, the pure and unmediated utterance of self. Thus, we tend to assume that even when we lie, the deception is always known to us and therefore purposefully delivered: it remains true to our hidden purposes. Writing in the conventional sense is comparatively evaluated against this notion of an unalienated self, or voice, and inevitably it is assumed to be a debasement of this prior moment, a supplementary, or later technology whose rearticulation brings the possibility of misrepresentations and distortions that escape our control. When we assume that the voice is (full of) pure intentionality and that what is heard within the shared moment of its phenomenological presence is self-referentially whole(some) and straightforwardly verifiable, then writing, inasmuch as it appears after and different from this event, will take on the qualities and capacities of an *external* violation of these initial conditions.

The point to be emphasized here is that what is interpreted as writing's moral failure is also taken as proof of its dangerous and more powerful achievement: the instrumental nature of its secondary and the calculating purchase of its parasitism. Writing is also regarded as an abstracting technology, something wherein the process of its "draw-ing out and away" exerts an effective transformation that takes an essential and pure ingredient and manufactures it into something else. What is especially provocative about the speech/writing split in this instance however, is that mathematical notation appears as an *originary writing*, an intimate alchemy where the power of abstraction is internal to its identity as the pure voice of reason itself. Thus, calculation becomes a virtue, a self-defined force that is unsullied by its context. Its integrity is therefore guaranteed because the direction and veracity of its calculations are not driven by personal motivation or situation but by something essentially selfless and uncontaminated by an interested subjectivity. With no person or agent involved, no*body* anchors its existential manifestation and, as a result, the truth of mathematical notation becomes the inexorable unfolding of a Natural calculation, incessantly reassessing and perfecting the accuracy of its measurements.

When mathematics appears as a measured discipline practiced by Nature itself, a *mathesis naturalis*, humankind is displaced from its central position as the original author and reasoning calculator. It is this removal of the person, the living, human agent of mathematical analysis that Rotman will contest. As the subtitle of one of his books makes clear, his strategy for this involves *Taking God Out of Mathematics and Putting the Body Back In.* However, Rotman's irritation with a "foundational hygiene" that escapes the situated contaminations of human perception, motivation, and fallibility becomes, ironically, a reaffirmation of its existence. Because if we read his argument closely we find that Rotman doesn't actually contest the idea of an a priori or original foundation, nor the corollary assumption that the stuff of this foundation provides necessary support for more complex architectures (writings and geometries). Indeed, he defines the human *against* the backdrop of Nature's enduring maintenance, as if the human arrives from outside the scene of its own production and as if that scene's inventive complexities in *conceiving* the human are entirely different from human *conceptual* capacities. This notion that a Natural realm of raw materials preexists Culture's mathematizations of it, such that the latter is derived yet separate from the former, is itself exemplary of phonocentrism and its hermetic enclosures. Phonocentrism effectively elides the *question* of temporality (sequence, causality, derivation) by assuming that the nature of relationality is self-evident in the representational morphology of linearity. But what is the stuff of this mysterious informational transfer that transcends difference while apparently preserving it?

The phonocentrism in Rotman's argument is underscored in his perception that the rigors of scriptibility that write "the rules, conventions, dictates, protocols, and such that control mathematical imagination" are not already at work in (what for the time being we will continue to call) Nature. Thus, a "foundational hygiene" is prerequisite to his insistence that the capacities and performative energies of abstraction, namely "writing," can be segregated from Nature. However, my point here is not so much to expand Rotman's project of inclusion, as if one might put the whole of Nature "back in" rather than just the human body, for I am instead trying to suggest that what Rotman understands the body or Nature to be is *already* that field of mathematical imagination and invention that his corrective would supplement.

How, then, might we acknowledge a *mathesis naturalis* whose arithmeticities already inform and motivate what Rotman might include? To broach this complexity we will need a more generous appreciation of why Rotman's desire for a "history of writing *as writing*" will be unable to either contain or explain the intricacies of the "gram" in terms of Culture. Interestingly, Rotman himself gestures in this direction when he struggles to envision what we might call the exuberant bodily connectivities that enable (why not say that are?) mathematical practice. "The understanding of writing appropriate to this conception of doing mathematics, what we might call *virtual writing*, would thus go beyond the 'archewriting' set out by Derrida, since it could no longer be conceived in terms of the 'gram' without wrenching that term out of all continuity with itself" (Rotman 1997, 37).

However and importantly, Derrida's "writing in the general sense," "grammatology" or "arche-writing," attempts to do just this! The graphematic structure supplements the notion of the "gram" as a visible sign with what we might call its other phenomenological and virtual possibilities. And yet it doesn't achieve this associational condensation by coupling one sense with another, as one might envisage the connecting links on a chain or even the different facets of a polygram—namely, this modality plus this one, and then this one too. More critically, it subverts the notion of "addition" (and therefore subtraction, division, multiplication) altogether, such that the gram's fundamental identity is, indeed, "out of all continuity with itself." The puzzle wherein each seemingly atomic identity resonates through webs of implication that are universally encompassing is not peculiar to quantum physics.

A simple illustration of this occurs quite routinely in arguments that rest on the spatial and temporal separation of Nature from Culture. Although such arguments (and we could take Rotman's as a case in point) regard these "systems" as ontologically discrete inasmuch as they are at pains to separate them, passing references to their mutual dependence may also be made. But how these supposedly *independent* spheres of influence are *dependent* and therefore ontologically compromised by their ability to effect and imply one another isn't explained. Surprisingly, the sense that there is something of a contradiction in such descriptions goes entirely unremarked.

When Einstein discovered evidence that our classical discriminations of the physical universe were unable to explain what he called "spooky action at a distance," a sort of haunting whereby the behavior of one entity seemed to animate or mirror another in ways that could not be explained in terms of speed of light communication (local causality), his skepticism that these findings actually coincided with reality didn't prevent him from acknowledging their apparent puzzle.[7] In the humanities, however, our investment in a physical reality whose substance must remain unaffected by our representations of it, a reality whose constancy and temporal priority preexist our conceptual idealizations, willfully ignores the radical implications and challenges in this work. There is an assumption that what happens in the physical sciences can have little to do with an analysis of the working components of literature, even though the questions we engage are often uncannily similar. Our intellectual energies are exercised by the chimerical nature of the analytical unit, the temporal impossibilities of an always/already that undermines causality, the mired relationship between ideation and materializing, lived realities, and so on. The paradoxes and indeterminacies in our arguments, indeterminacies that confound the classical distinction between Nature and Culture (substance and form), even subject and object, are explained in terms of the circumscribed processes of linguistics and representation. In other words, *secondary* technologies are thought to engender distortions and errors in the representation of reality's presumptive stability—its *original* objects and processes. When we resolve the riddles that confront us through a logic of representationalism, we reinvest in the speech/writing, presence/absence divisions that we criticize elsewhere.[8]

The provocations in Derrida's early work regarding the implications of a general writing, or what we might call an "inclusive systematicity," have been considerably restricted in the humanities through disciplinary adjudication.[9] However, if Nature's purported *pre*-scriptions are not the fixed and immutable lessons that we inherit, if they do not precede us but are contemporary articulations of the evolving and involved complexity which we are, what difference does it make? If, following and elaborating the themes in Derrida's early work we at least entertain the notion that the gram may include much more than the atom of classical thought, appearing as a quantum "entity" whose apparently tiny dimensions have universal resonance, then we are provided with a more workable account of a *mathesis generalis*, and one that doesn't sustain the conservatism that usually accompanies naturalizing arguments.

As this is quite a mouthful to digest, this part of my argument requires careful exegesis. First, there can be no controversy in the statement that mathematics figures. As the Latin derivation suggests—*fingere*—to form, shape; *la figura*—a form. Mathematics draws lines between things, implicitly and explicitly. And those lines can be as problematic as the entities they appear to connect, fracture, or produce. Yet there is something within mathematics, and as we will see, something internal to all recognizable writing systems, that denies the tangled involvement or wild geometries of their internal processes, processes that constitute the very ontogenesis of their "presenting"—their legibility. If we return to Rotman's explanation of how mathematics achieves a quite successful obfuscation of its representational dimensions we will recall that he drew diagnostic purchase from alphabeticism. Alphabeticism enables something that mathematics needs, while also providing an effective defense against something that mathematics rejects. Although the stabilizing anchor can be the unfolding of speech, the voice of subjective intention, in more general terms it is the unmediated reality, or referent, whose haecceity speech instantiates. Because "the familiar authority of the alphabetic text" (Rotman 1997, 32) is so easily taken as the definitive stuff of writing, the "how and what it is" (1997, 32), it follows that mathematical grams can appear as if from nowhere, a "writing" that is pre- or nonlinguistic.

If we pause at this point, it is apparent that the substantive difference between one writing form and another, or the reason why each is regarded as autological, remains confused. Several examples will illustrate this. Let us begin with Rotman's description of the phobic response of literature to a different expression of writing. Rotman argues that "alphabetic writing achieves the closure of a false completeness, a self-sufficiency in which the fear of mathematical signs that motivates it is rendered as invisibly as the grams themselves" (1997, 32). Rotman also notes the dearth of schematic visual representation outside the sciences and ponders why words are imbued with such self-sufficiency, as if the subject matter could never stray. He notes, "Diagrams of any kind are so rare in the texts produced by historians, philosophers, and literary theorists, among others, that any instance sticks out like a sore thumb . . . isn't the refusal to use figures, arrows, vectors, and so forth, as modes of explication part of the very basis on which the humanities define themselves as different from the technosciences?" (1997, 30).

Although Rotman makes a really interesting point here and I don't wish to diminish its validity (indeed I want to take it further), he stops short of exploring its inverse implications. Why, for example, are the visual geometries, the individual morphologies of alphabetic letters, so effectively invisibilized that they are not included in this notion of "visual representation" and "diagram?" Why is a letter such as "p" for example, a letter that is itself a diagram, something written or marked out by lines, deemed more *intrinsically* sayable than the diagram "Δ"?[10] When the grapheme is rendered invisible it follows that we will not ponder the process that enables a phoneme (and let's assume here something we would all recognize as sayable) to become visible; to resemble and be a grapheme in the conventional sense. In sum, how can an exterior and completely different representation of what was originally a sayable entity claim to be derived from that entity, and somehow be different and yet same? Or, as Derrida remarks in one of his many attempts to expose the knot of contradictions in phonocentrism, "Does not the radical dissimilarity of the two elements—graphic and phonic—exclude derivation?" (1984, 54).

We can use Rotman's own description here, but with a different application, and ask how mathematical notation is able to derive its considerable status from the "closure of a false completeness, a self-sufficiency," which in this case defines numericism against writing/the alphabet? After all, the alphabet's many combinatorial possibilities involve a "coming to count," or *valeur* as Saussure calls it, which is not a simple synonym for meaning in the ordinary sense. Indeed, as cryptography makes evident, the intimate connection between mathematics and literature is substantial. The differential of spacing and timing, with its internal additions, subtractions, divisions, and multiplications of diacritical potentialities, is an algebra—the patternment of "broken-ness." What underwrites the connectivities in apparently different systems, and in such a way that linearity, as well as the integrity of these systems, are profoundly disrupted and universally dispersed?

As I try to make this point I am reminded of an exercise I occasionally undertake with my students. I have presented them with sonograms, sheets of Braille, Burmese inscriptions, voice prints from patients with cancer of the larynx and without it, lie detector results, hieroglyphs, aboriginal sand paintings, Boolean printouts, the electromagnetic bands of gene sequences, messages in Morse code, and more. Of course, this can be extended to the pheromone trails of ants, to what happens in the grafting of different plants, or in the syntax of the atomic tables. My aim in assembling this mélange of images is that their unfamiliarity will provoke several questions. What are the essential ingredients in these "organisms" (the etymology of this word is suggestive) whose machinery allows them to work? What makes each of these different systems coherent and individual, and yet translatable into forms that appear to have absolutely no relationship to them? What is legibility when you really get down to it? What, after all, do all these combinatorial "patternments" share that explain their common status as "language"? If we pose these questions honestly we can see why the intimate knowledge we have of how our own natural language works may actually conceal the puzzle's real challenge and difficulty. Meaning and reference may appear self-evident, the explanatory anchors of language. Yet this simple exercise asks us to reconsider the solidity of these stabilizing points, and once we've done this, the independence of numerical and linguistic representation, or even that of geometry, is compromised.

When Rotman presumes that mathematics is a uniquely human technology he attempts to infect Platonism's timelessness with the human contaminations of a cultural and historical context. And it is this corporeally anchored and situated context, this "empirically derived basis for the application of mathematics *to* the world" (Rotman, 1993a, 142; my emphasis) that explains its "unreasonable effectiveness." And so it is that the body's natural immersion in "empirically originated patterns, processes, and regularities" (1993a, 142) previews the abstractions of mathematics proper. And yet we are still left with a question about the communicative effectiveness between mind and body, and between the inside and outside of the body, a question whose terms are repeated when we consider the body's internal arithmetic: what language operates *between* perceptual patterns and regularities to realize experiential coherence? What arithmetic allows the body's internal differentiations to make sense, whereby what appears as "one" modality can translate to, or anticipate its difference from, another, and finesse discrepancies? I want to argue that the body's "situation" must *be* these involvements, even though their communicative resonances confound the coordinates of a simple "here" and "now": this carnal implication, or sensate interiority, expresses a geometry that eschews division and yet relies upon its discriminations.

Perception is a thesis of ongoing action wherein interpretive negotiations abstract coherence in disconnection and vice versa. And yet despite the complexity in this achievement, the processes of perception are commonly segregated from those of intellection. When we assume that perception involves techniques that are quite different from reading/writing, perhaps granting that perception's operations subtend abstraction as their mere vehicle, or that they provide the inchoate data that are later organized and interpreted, we ignore the inherent literacy of this cooperative functionality. For what is reading if it isn't a perceptual discrimination whose mechanism is an intricate immersion technology? The point is an elusive one, and it is habitually denied in its most forceful affirmation, as we see when Rotman argues that doing mathematics is a corporeal practice. For it is quite clear that Rotman does not mean by this that the body's own engagement with/in itself is a mathematical practice. Instead, he understands the body in Cartesian terms as an object akin to an avatar or vehicle, a container that enables calculation to be done by a subject/person who pilots it. Accordingly, carnality cannot *be* calculating and thinking material through and through, any more than the subject *is* the body's changing situations. Thus, a person might well practice mathematics *upon* the body, or *with* its help, but apparently it is not in the nature of corporeality to mathematize, represent, or intelligently take measure of itself.

Rotman's argument about the specific ontology of mathematics is mobilized in terms of an inside/outside architecture that inadvertently succumbs to the mirror-maze of a secret geometry. To explain this, we will recall that for Rotman the mistake in the Platonic view of mathematics was to locate the realm of number in an elsewhere quite outside the human condition: it follows that the question of its origins inevitably "invok[es] a deity (the source of the miraculous 'gift')." Against this view of a transcendent and decontextualized mathematics Rotman discovers its true source in the grounded, corporeal situation of the human condition: thus, mathematics is not a gift from God but an accomplishment of the perceptual experience that makes it possible. However, Rotman's acknowledgment of perception as a sort of proto-mathematics continues to separate its apparently raw and undigested "figures" from the calculations of conscious reasoning. Inevitably, the phonocentrism of this speech/writing split must ontologize the subject who calculates and exerts control *over* these processes as different from those processes. But where does Rotman's subject reside? Apparently, on the other side of Nature, for if Nature, or the nonhuman, could abstract, then a form of Platonic theology, something that appears to displace the human from the center of the world as its interpreting architect, might be reincarnated. Would such a possibility simply recuperate Platonic thought or, by reworking its terms of reference, could it herald a "miraculous gift" that is as alive and necessary to the impetus behind Rotman's argument as to Platonic transcendentalism?

Before considering these questions perhaps we need to be a little clearer about the "terms of reference" mentioned above. Let us consider Rotman's understanding of the body in this regard, with its "empirically originated

patterns, processes, and regularities." To think through the body and acknowledge its contextual relevance for mathematics we might ask how
Rotman draws a qualitative distinction between perceptual cipherings and
the transcriptions, encryptions, and translations we call letter and number.
How is intellection distilled from the intrigue of biological performativities,
or more provocatively still, why aren't they one and the same? Why is the
belief that the body is "given" to us as something that preexists its cultural
interpretation assumed to be so very different from the theological commitments in Platonic thought that Rotman denounces? Do we resolve the
mystery of mathematics that the phrase "miraculous gift" acknowledges
when we contest its divine source by underlining its corporeal situation?

Rotman's fixation with making the gram visible provides us with an
opportunity to pause and actually think about the corporeal intelligence of
perception and experience. Although vision certainly seems to be a sensory
modality among others, its actual operation has synaesthetic amplitude
that betrays simple identification. If we consider the conversational dimensions of the optic nerve as an example of this, then the language of light and
electricity would be intrinsic to Rotman's argument about the gram's visibility. But what happens to our notion of visibility when we acknowledge
the biological processes whose translations make it manifest? Our blood
can race at the mere sight of someone. Can blood see? Does the retina
organize and narrativize light and energy into significance? Does energy
remember? If we explain away such questions by attributing their strange-
ness to poetic license or mere metaphor we discount the workings of
biological poiesis. What is happening when I speak on the phone without
my glasses and find that I can't hear as clearly? Do I merely imagine my
incapacity, or is "one" modality always/already re-calling the "other"? And
if I do "merely" imagine, then again, why is this not a biological phenomenon of/with material manifestation?

Elizabeth Wilson's discussion of Elaine Showalter's work on conversion
hysteria is especially provocative in teasing out this last point because
Wilson uncovers an enduring somatophobia in arguments whose stated
aim is to repair the neglect, denigration, or exile of the body from knowledge production. Interestingly, although Wilson's argument is a disruption
of feminist preconceptions, it can be argued that it more generously confirms their motivating political energies and directions, but with a degree
of rigor that is often abandoned in the heat of accusation and diagnosis.

Wilson's question, given its quite extraordinary ramifications, is surprisingly simple: "We may be well equipped to answer *why* hysterics convert, but we appear to be collectively mute in response to the question of *how* they convert" (1999, 10). Wilson refers us to the remarkable example of Augustine, Jean-Martin Charcot's most famous patient in the Salpêtrière hospital of the late nineteenth century, as an exemplary instance of such "oversights." "Among [Augustine's] gifts was her ability to time and divide her hysterical performances into scenes, acts, tableaux, and intermissions, to perform on cue and on schedule with the click of a camera. But Augustine's cheerful willingness to assume whatever poses her audience desired took its toll on her psyche. During the period when she was being repeatedly photographed, she developed a curious hysterical symptom: she began to see everything in black and white" (10).

Showalter's rush to deliver a "unidimensional narrative of victimisation (photographed, anaesthetized, locked up)" (Wilson 1999, 11) discovers the cause of these symptoms in Charcot's dehumanizing desires and insensitivities. Clearly, Augustine the person is quite invisible. However, Wilson argues that Showalter's need to satisfy her own analytical desires by discussing the hidden agenda that explains these symptoms represents yet another cancellation of Augustine's reality. If Charcot objectifies Augustine's antique postures, Showalter chooses to look right past them, not even pausing to remark on the woman's quite extraordinary representational capacities. As Wilson explains, "By passing over the biology of conversion, Showalter does not simply miss some of the most compelling questions about Augustine's hysteria, she also places the nature of human biology outside the orbit of feminist analysis. Her anecdote renders the retina, the optic nerve and the brain psychologically inert and politically barren—mere ciphers for a cultural (read: non-biological) force that is located *elsewhere*" (1999, 11). Could Augustine's performance, with its rebus of intersubjective, psychological, biological, and even machinic connections with the camera, *be* a "gram" whose expressive possibility Rotman mused about, a "gram" whose wild geometry, "wrench[ed] . . . out of all continuity with itself," is the saturation of the sensible?[11]

I have noted several times that Rotman understands perception as "empirically originated patterns, processes, and regularities." And here I am reminded of Keith Devlin's definition of mathematics that opened this discussion—*"the science of order, patterns, structure, and logical relation-*

ships." My question is this; why are the patterns or differentiations that Rotman might regard as "empirically originated," patterns that "re-cognize" themselves and each other in order to function, excluded from his understanding of reading and writing? Rotman seems to concede that while the body may be mathematical in essence, it does not have the calculating energy to *do* mathematics. However, if what we conventionally call Nature is as actively literate, numerate, and inventive as anything we might include within Culture—witness the phenomenon of conversion hysteria, or more simply, perception itself—then what is the makeup of this segregating division? Or, for the sake of argument, if we grant that there are indeed separate realms of activity, then how are their distinctive differences effectively synthesized?

As my argument hails biology here in order to provoke a reconsideration of relationality (between Culture and Nature; thought/language/ideality and perception/matter/visceral intuition), and as Rotman also acknowledges that work on the neuronal activity of cognition might help to complicate this whole puzzle, it might be instructive to close this discussion by illustrating, again, how these provocations can quickly lose energy if they are not sustained.

In *Conversations on Mind, Matter, and Mathematics* (1995) Alain Connes, a mathematician at the Collège de France, debates Jean-Pierre Changeux, a neurobiologist from the same institution.[12] Changeux's irritation with Connes hinges on the latter's Platonic abstraction: Changeux believes that mathematical reality is a peculiarly human reality, a cultural invention, and therefore something whose insights are derived from human endeavor. However, something peculiar happens when Changeux locates this achievement in terms of the *human* brain, as if biology's capacities in general are identified and circumscribed, or even erased, by the adjective "human." If invention and creativity are biological energies, then surely Nature's apparent passivity in the face of Culture's agency is a misguided dichotomy. What do we lose if we think of biology as a "unified field" of operational differentiations, a *mathesis naturalis?* Clearly, if I inject into Nature the sense of mutation, possibility, and yet structured movement that is normally ascribed to Culture, then a *mathesis naturalis* is not a fixed *pre*-scription but an evolving and implicate calculation. And if I find in this "field" the question of the subject— albeit a subject who seizes upon itself as an object newly discovered—then the measured considerations of this self-discovery might constitute a re*invention.*

Exteriority then, would be but a fold in interiority as it explores and digests its own difference. In such a scene, the Platonic insistence that mathematics is somehow discovered, appearing to precede inquiry and human creation, would not exclude the possibility that it is *also* fabricated in the synchrony of what appears at that same moment of discovery. This involvement breathes life and a different dimension into an aside made by Derrida about related issues: "Between rationalism and mysticism there is, then, a certain complicity" (1984, 80).

4. Natural Convers(at)ions

Or, What If Culture Was Really Nature All Along?

～

The Linguistic Turn—Culture Takes Precedence

The "linguistic turn" in postmodern and poststructural criticism has had a major impact on the landscape of the humanities and social sciences and the way we conceive and communicate our various concerns. Words such as "text," "writing," "inscription," "discourse," "language," "code," "representation," and so on are now part of the vernacular in critical discussion. Indeed, over the years the textualizing of objects and methodologies has generated new interdisciplinary formations across the academy and transformed the content, approach, and even the justifications for research. On the political front we have seen similar shifts in the practices, modes of argumentation, and even the alliances and strategies that once identified particular social movements and struggles for equity. And all this because the material self-evidence of initial conditions or first causes, those stable analytical reference points that allow us to identify a problem and then debate what needs to be done to correct it, have suffered a significant assault. Although in a very real sense political contestation has always debated first principles, once the substantive difference between Nature and Culture, or temporal priority and causal directionality, is disestablished, we enter a very different zone of political possibility.

The following meditation will revisit what has surely been a truism for cultural criticism, namely, the need to interrogate the Nature/Culture division and the entire conceptual apparatus that rests upon it. Although one might be forgiven for assuming that the insights we can glean from such an examination have been exhausted, the aim of this chapter is to illuminate the more counterintuitive and surprising aspects of this problematic that could open new and unusual avenues for critical attention. Why they are routinely overlooked is a curious phenomenon in itself because the evidence I want to bring to the discussion is neither hidden nor missing, but patently manifest. For this reason we will give some consideration to why these particular provocations have been elided, and perhaps more profoundly, we will ask why their very possibility should prove so unthinkable.

This analysis will draw on one of the genetic markers of a certain style of feminist and cultural criticism, namely, the critique of Cartesian thought and the political inflections that pivot around its binary logic. Theorists of gender, sexuality, and race, for example, have found that Nature/the body is routinely conflated with woman, the feminine, the primordial, with wild passion and "the dark continent"—all signs of a primitive deficiency that requires a more rational and evolved presence (the masculine/whiteness/ heterosexuality/Culture and civilization) to control and direct its unruly potential. The value of this work is not in dispute here, indeed, in a very real sense my argument will try to extend the more intricate and productive aspects of its insights. Nevertheless, the immediate task is to understand why, on closer inspection, the strategies for overturning the automatic denigration of Nature and the battery of devaluations associated with it have remained wedded to its repetition.

As this is a big claim it is best approached in small steps, steps that will retrace our commitments to some foundational building blocks. Let us begin with the problem of binary oppositions in order to understand why this logic might enable Cartesianism as well as the arguments in cultural criticism that strive to overturn it. It is somewhat routine within critical discourse, for example, to diagnose binary oppositions as if they are pathological symptoms—conceptual errors that are enduring, insidious, and whose effects can normalize political inequity. If the remedial treatment for such symptoms is to replace these binary errors with nonbinary correctives, however, then surely we are caught in something of a quandary. In other words, if every maneuver to escape binary logic effectively reinstates it in a disavowed and subtle way, then perhaps we need a more careful examination of what we are actually dealing with in this mirror-maze of unwitting duplication.

To take just one facet of the binarity riddle, we might wonder whether the difference that renders entities autonomous and therefore distinct from others is a true reflection of their actual independence and separateness. This seems like a straightforward question, yet one of the insights in semiology is that when we identify something and attribute it with its very own meaning and properties we arrive at this determination through a web of sticky associations that corrupt its claim to autonomy. The co-responding resonances that animate language and perception actually determine (some might say produce) particularity, and this is why certain poststructural accounts of identity formation argue that context, an external difference, is also constitutively and operationally interior to the identity it seems to surround. Following this logic, if we commit to the notion of difference as an internal ingredient within identity formation rather than an external "in-between" separate identities, should we then conclude that seemingly different identities are "somehow" inseparable rather than autonomous? The real curiosity appears at this juncture: we are now unable to make a simple discrimination between separability and inseparability, as we have just conceded that the riddle of identity confounds the very terms that might allow us to answer this question. All terms within a binary opposition, including the term "difference," are now profoundly compromised and entangled. Indeed, even the discrimination of any *one* term (this is identifiable because it isn't something else) cannot escape this knot of implication.

As discussions of the Cartesian body/mind (Nature/Culture) division so often illustrate, the more counterintuitive and potentially productive dimensions of the binary puzzle that query the very makeup of the categories can often disappear in the diagnostic moralism of critique: instead of acknowledging that the very stuff of the body and the processes that purportedly separate thought from carnality are now something of a mystery, if they exist at all, the essence of these "components" and their connections can be taken for granted. There is little risk in most contemporary criticism, for example, of attributing agency and intelligent inventiveness (Culture) to the capacities of flesh and matter (Nature). Or if this is conceded in certain information and system theories, a line of political demarcation, a sense of what is interior to one system versus what is exterior and other in another, will inadvertently recuperate the Nature/Culture division in a different form.[1] In sum, Nature is deemed to be thoughtless—either relatively or absolutely—and political interventions into Cartesian logic are much more likely to preserve this assumption by expanding the category "Culture" to transform and textualize whatever it is defined against. If the myriad manifestations of Nature are actually mediations or re-presentations, that is, second-order signs of cultural invention, then Nature, as such, is absent.

Although these analytical strategies represent crucial points of entry into the more fascinating implications of this problematic, it becomes clear that both Cartesianism and its critique are entirely committed to maintaining the difference between Nature and Culture, presence and absence, and matter and form. Arguing that we remain indebted to the materiality of the body, that we are always attached to it and never independent of it, that both women and men are equally corporeal, or that none of us can *properly* be identified with Nature's primordial insufficiency if this determination is a political (Cultural) one, doesn't in any way dislodge the premise of Cartesianism as it is commonly received.[2] In all of these arguments it goes without saying that Nature/the body/materiality preexists Culture/intellect/abstraction, and furthermore, that the thinking self is not an articulation of matter's intentions. Given this, what we will need to keep at the forefront of this meditation is whether the conventional sense of difference as something that divides identities from each other—materiality *from* abstraction—or, similarly, something that joins materiality *to* abstraction (because we still assume in this case that two different things are connected) can adequately acknowledge the riddle of identity.[3]

But let us return to the Nature/Culture division to consider how this particular example of identity that presumes opposition is commonly explained in cultural and feminist theoretical writings. In the main, it is now axiomatic to eschew naturalizing arguments for several reasons. First and perhaps most important, they are regarded as inherently conservative. Compared with the cacophony of cultural explanations that exemplify contestation, movement, and change, it follows that natural determinations will seem like a prescriptive return to something from the past, something deemed to be undeniable and immutable. In the former case, when we explain our thoughts and actions as cultural products and effects we are also emphasizing that we are active agents in our political destinies. By embracing the notion of natural cause and determination, however, we run the risk of reducing what seems so special about the human condition to evolutionary happenstance, or Nature's caprice. When we really get down to it, it is the essential nature and special complexity of *human* being that is at stake in these debates.

The assumption that the threat of Nature can be put aside in some way has been justified theoretically by the linguistic turn itself, which promotes the belief that Culture is an enclosed system of significations, representations, and codes that afford us no immediate access to Nature at all. According to this view and as already noted above, cultural webs of interpretation that include linguistic and even perceptual frames of legibility are intricately enmeshed and cross-referenced, and this raft of mediations stands between any direct experience or knowledge of Nature's raw facticity. Consequently, the difference between cultural and natural facts is impossible to adjudicate, and this is why we inevitably and necessarily confuse cultural constructions of nature with "Nature itself."

When Scientific Objects Turn into Language

A clear illustration of the view that it is in the nature of Culture to unwittingly take itself for Nature is evident in the following example. In an interview with Judith Butler, whose work is well known for its analytical commitment to cultural constructionism (albeit a very complex and nuanced form that assumes its inevitability and is therefore wary of naive correctives), I took the opportunity to ask if the organizing trope in her work, namely, language, discourse—textuality—had been too narrowly conceived. My question was inspired by medical and scientific research that claims to investigate the brute reality of material objects and processes: why does the essential nature of these scientific objects also appear to be textual? Within the sciences, the stuff of the body appears as codes, signs, transcriptions, and signatures—language systems and mathematical algorithms. In the cognitive sciences, for example, it seems that explanations of neural-net behavior, or how neurons learn new material through an inherent plasticity and interactionism (in other words, any "one" neuron is already "webbed"), parallel Ferdinand de Saussure's explication of the peculiar associational resonances that inform any unit of the language system.[4] Other useful comparisons have been made between the communicative structures of biological languages and the language theories of Charles Sanders Peirce,[5] and Jacques Derrida acknowledged that the puzzle of language is just as evident in cybernetics and the biological sciences as it is in literature and philosophy.[6] Even the layperson is increasingly aware that biological information in general, from genetic structures to the translation capacities of our immune system, shares some workable comparison with natural languages. But what are these languages, these biological grammars that seem to be the communicative stuff of life?

Admittedly, we do not tend to think of signs as *substantively* or ontologically material, and yet, what prevents us from doing so remains unclear. With such considerations in mind I directed the following question to Judith Butler: "There is a serious suggestion that 'life itself' is creative encryption. Does your understanding of language and discourse extend to the workings of biological codes and their apparent intelligence?" (Kirby in Breen et al. 2001, 13). On this last point I was thinking of the code-cracking and encryption capacities of bacteria as they decipher the chemistry of antibiotic data and reinvent themselves accordingly. Aren't these language skills?

Butler's response is a form of admonition, a reminder that language is circumscribed, that its author and reader is human, and that the human endeavor to capture a world "out there" through cultural signs will always be a failed project. To this end, she warns:

There are models according to which we might try to understand biology, and models by which we might try to understand how genes function. And in some cases the models are taken to be inherent to the phenomena that is [*sic*] being explained. Thus, Fox-Keller has argued that certain computer models used to explain gene sequencing in the fruit fly have recently come to be accepted as intrinsic to the gene itself. I worry that a notion like "biological code," on the face of it, runs the risk of that sort of conflation. I am sure that encryption can be used as a metaphor or model by which to understand biological processes, especially cell reproduction, but do we then make the move to render what is useful as an explanatory model into the ontology of biology itself? This worries me, especially when it is mechanistic models which lay discursive claims on biological life. What of life exceeds the model? When does the discourse claim to become the very life it purports to explain? I am not sure it is possible to say "life itself" is creative encryption unless we make the mistake of thinking that the model is the ontology of life.

Indeed, we might need to think first about the relation of any definition of life to life itself, and whether it must, by virtue of its very task, fail. (Butler in Breen et al. 2001, 13)

Butler is understandably vigilant about the seductive slide that conflates representations, models, and signs that substitute for material objects, with the objects themselves. In other words, although it is inevitable that we will misrecognize one in the other, Butler cautions against committing to the error. When dealing with scientific objects the transparent self-evidence of reality is even more persuasive, but even here we are encouraged to remember that these objects are actually literary—textual, or encoded forms of language—and to this extent, if they can only emerge through cultural manufacture, then their reality and truth is attenuated, or even illusional.

Although this argument is certainly persuasive, especially against the sort of hard-edged empiricist and positivist scientific claims that give little consideration to how the vagaries of interpretation might effect material results, there are lingering problems nevertheless. If we contextualize Butler's intervention in terms of the political legacy of binarity mentioned earlier, she effectively challenges the devaluation of Nature (the feminine, matter, the origin) by arguing that these significations are cultural ascriptions with no *essential* truth. If the economy of valuation can be analyzed, contested, and redistributed (because this is the operational definition of Culture), then the question of Nature is *entirely* displaced; put simply, it can have no frame of reference that is properly its own, for even the concept/word "Nature" must evoke meanings, prejudices, and perceptions that are learned.

To accept that we are bound within the enclosure of Culture is to commit to a raft of related assumptions, and although there is certainly some interpretive play in what we make of them it might be helpful to register something of their broad outline here. The most important is the assertion that *humanness is profoundly unnatural.* The abstracting technology of language, intelligence, and creative invention is separated from the body of the material world, indeed, even from the material body of human animality. Ironically, given the initial concern to question the separation of Nature from Culture within Cartesianism, the sense that human identity is somehow secured and enclosed against a more primordial and inhuman "outside" (which must include the subject's own corporeal being!) recuperates the Cartesian problematic, but this time without the enduring questions that continued to trouble Descartes. Given this, it is not surprising that cultural arguments that relentlessly interrogate the autonomy and integrity of identity formation fall mute when it comes to the question of how Culture conceives and authenticates its own special properties and self-sufficiency. If we translate the separation of Culture from Nature into the mind/body split, it seems that the Cartesian subject can admit that s/he has a body (that *attaches* to the self), and yet s/he is somehow able to sustain the belief that *s/he is not this body.* This denial is necessary because to contest the latter and all its possible consequences would at least suggest that it might be in the nature of the biological body to argue, reinvent, and rewrite itself—to reflect on itself and cogitate.

Neither Descartes, nor any cultural critic who draws analytical purchase from some version of the linguistic turn, would deny that human identity incorporates two quite different systems of endeavor. Not many would dispute the presence of a biological reality that is quite different from Culture and that we imperfectly try to comprehend. But surely, if we were without our skin and we could witness the body's otherwise invisible pro-cesses as we chat to each other, read a presentation aloud, type away at our computers, or negotiate an intense exchange with someone we care about, we might be forced to acknowledge that perhaps the meat of the body *is* thinking material. If it is in the nature of biology to be cultural—and clearly, what we mean by "cultural" is intelligent, capable of interpreting, analyzing, reflecting, and creatively reinventing and memorializing—then what is this need to exclude such processes of interrogation from the ontology of life? The difference between ideality and matter, models and what they purportedly represent, or signs of life and life itself, is certainly difficult to separate here. However, it is important to emphasize that this confusing implication cannot be corrected in the way that Butler attempts to do. Although her work underlines why there will always be confusion, she explains this blurring of object and interpretation as an inevitable mistake that derives from the exceptionalism of the human condition—the hermetic enclosure of the interpretive enterprise, or mind itself.

Entangling the Question of Language/System

Two different considerations arise at this juncture that assist in pushing the problematic forward instead of reiterating the normative frame of reference that has become somewhat routine in cultural criticism. In passing, we might note that in a very different field of inquiry the implication between concepts (ideality) and things (materiality), or interpretive intent and material behavior, in quantum relations, is so profound that it undermines our understanding of their respective differences. As we might imagine, there are just as many interpretive arguments among physicists and philosophers today about the significance of quantum "weirdness," as Einstein called it, as we see in the broad community of poststructural and cultural criticism. However, to risk a comparison, what binds all of us is a sense that the way the world works isn't at all straightforward, and that counterintuitive approaches to questions about communication between senders and receivers, or more comprehensively, individuals of whatever sort, whether atoms, measuring instruments, human subjects—"phenomena" more generally[7]—might have more explanatory power than what seems unequivocally and banally self-evident.

Even those of us outside the sciences are aware of something surprising about the nature of light and its ability to assume different forms—wave or particle—a dispersed manifestation or one that appears local. This shift in expression is especially remarkable when we grant that its particular manifestation is "somehow" caught up with the choice of measuring apparatus. However, as Karen Barad makes clear, and this point is of crucial importance for my argument, if the different parts of the experiment—the object under investigation, the inquiring scientist, and the apparatus—are "entangled," then this does not mean that there are three different "entities" interacting with each other. Entanglement suggests that the very ontology of the entities emerges *through* relationality: the entities do not preexist their involvement. As odd as it may seem, this also implies that the "original" intention to perform the experiment, to inquire, is not a capacity that can therefore be attributed to a human inquirer, as we might assume. Not unrelated is the way we identify temporal differences as past, present, and future, for example, when we assume that the scientist initiates an experiment that a photon is *then* subjected to. Such linear notions of causal unfolding can appear "synchronized" on the quantum level, occurring in "no time" (the meaning of these words is deformed) when such experiments appear to anticipate what will have already taken place. Remarkably, the results of such experiments are retrospectively actualized and empirically verifiable.[8] Is the weirdness of this evidence rendered explicable because it reflects the epistemological intertextualities—the criss-crossings of what can only be metaphors and models, whose cultural origins have little if anything to do with the actualities of the universe at large? Or is there a more worldly form of intratextual referencing in these scientific results that collapse concept (model), observer, and observed, and disperse authorship, identity, and causality?

To underline the unpredictable and quite odd complexities in this question we need to appreciate why there is a sense that the choice of experimental measurement is somehow delayed, or "too late," because the actual manifestation of the photon must surely be evident, or already "itself," prior to this choice. Or to put this another way, it seems quite impossible that the choice of measurement can retrospectively anticipate and actively materialize what one would have thought was already existent. The dilemma here is that our attempts to describe the strange outcome of this experiment can inadvertently ignore the mysterious sense of entanglement, or intra-action, in the operational possibility of this "event."[9] There is a temporal configuration in the above description's narrative order that preserves the logic of causal separation and the presumption that there are different moments in time, different places in space, and a very real difference between thought and material reality. To suggest that one affects or interferes with the other in a way that renders them inseparable doesn't confound the nature of their difference (respective identities) so much as it emphasizes that these differences are joined or connected in some way. In the first instance, we interpret "inseparability" to mean that human agency and intention produced a change in the nature of reality and that this is proof of some mysterious connection between them. The very same logic would allow us to reverse the direction of this causal explanation to suggest that some agential force in the universe directed humans to conduct an experiment whose results the world had already anticipated. However, neither of these explanations captures the sheer wonder of the spacetime entanglement at work here, even though this last reversal begins to trouble the properties that we tend to attribute to these different identities (human *and* nonhuman, mind *and* phenomenon) and the relational asymmetries that affirm the difference in their properties, capacities, and timings.

If we consider these implications more carefully, then significance and substance, thought and matter, human agency and material objectivity, must be consubstantial. But what does this actually mean and can we do anything interesting with such a wild assertion? Of course, the linguist Ferdinand de Saussure said something very similar about the consubstantiality of semiological association when he tried to capture the weight, or *valeur*, that rendered the linguistic unit workable; and Judith Butler's more contemporary interpretation of his argument insists that signification matters and that ideation can real-ize. In other words, many of the most important interventions in cultural criticism that condense differences together seem to conjure with similar counterintuitive assertions. Our question here, however, is whether these insights *only* relate to the peculiar attributes of Culture. To return to the specific question of scientific modeling, must we assume that these models are interpretive illusions produced by humans to mirror (and inevitably distort) a world that cannot be accessed? Because if they are mere illusions and the world is not present *in* them, then how can they possess the extraordinary capacity (as we see in the case of quantum relations) to anticipate verifiable outcomes whose pragmatic results are evident in such achievements as the computing and electronic technologies of contemporary life? As the philosopher Wesley C. Salmon insists after providing a list of justificatory proofs for the theory, "Quantum mechanics has had more explanatory success than any other theory in the history of science" (quoted in Norris 1997, 16–17).

It seems that the little steps by which we retraced our way to certain foundational commitments about binarity and the nature of language very quickly turned into the most baffling puzzles about the nature of life and the mysteries of the universe! And while the complexities of scientific theory surely exceed our disciplinary expertise, the discussion above has made the appeal to an "absolute outside" of anything, whether the discipline of physics, or indeed, theories of textual interpretation for that matter, considerably more fuzzy. For this reason, and in the spirit of a more meditative style of inquiry, perhaps we can at least risk the suggestion that if the quantum conflation of *thesis* with/in *physis* has general purchase, then we should not read the most complex aspects of poststructuralism as pure *thesis*. The most counterintuitive arguments about the superposition of matter and ideation, concept and object; all of the close analytical criticism that discovers systems of referral and relationality *within* identity/ the individual; the peculiar spacetime condensations that we confront in Freud's notion of memory or *Nachträglichkeit* (deferred action); or the "intra-actions" of Derridean *différance* and its counterintuitive implications—need we assume that such insights are purely "cultural" because the world itself, in its enduring insistence, simply could not be that dynamically involved and alien to ordinary commonsense?

Perhaps we should stick to something more straightforward that will test the conventional interpretation of cultural constructionism just as effectively by showing that a precritical understanding of reference as something self-evident in Nature is inadequately countered by theories of the referent as a cultural artifact. The question is disarmingly simple, so simple that one has to wonder why such questions are so rarely asked within the disciplinary protocols of cultural criticism; namely, can the rampant culturalism that understands the mediations of language as a purely cultural technology, a technology that *cannot* have any substantial purchase because it remains enclosed against itself, explain the efficacy of computational models, biograms of skin prints, blood evidence, genetic signatures, pollen chemistries, and insect life cycles (all data that present as languages)? How can this cacophony of differences possess *any* possibility of predictive reference? As we are well aware from forensic investigation techniques, data is indicative. From global networks of information that bring geology, biology, psychology, entomology, cryptography, and even the very personal street smarts of a particular observing investigator or profiler into conversation and convergence, a referent is thrown up. The most obvious question that this intricate process raises is—how?

Quantum Implications and the Practice of Critique

The reluctance of postmodern styles of criticism to actively consider how scientific models of Nature work at all (even when imperfectly, but certainly when we witness their extraordinary predictive accuracy) has lead many to discount the productive energy in these theories without appreciating what they can actually offer. Bruno Latour for example, a sociologist and historian of science, pours vitriol upon those "gloating" cultural constructivists whose smug self-enclosure attributes all agency and articulation to a brain in a vat (1999, 8). With considerable irritation he rails against the idea that anyone could celebrate musing blindly about a world that can no longer be accessed from the confines of a linguistic prison house. To paraphrase Latour's position, such arguments descend further and further into the same dark and spiraling curves of the same hell that is Cartesianism—"We have not moved an inch" (8).

As a prominent figure in the field of science studies,[10] a field that draws much of its analytical energy from cultural studies and cultural criticism more generally, Latour's position is an awkward one: he has to marry what he sees as the intrinsic value of empirical research in the sciences with his own discipline's attention to the subjective, historical, and cultural inflections of knowledge production. The way he does this is to refuse reality an "ahistorical, isolated, inhuman, cold, objective existence" (1999, 15). Accordingly, Latour shifts his attention from objects and claims to objectivity, to the messy business of scientific practice, or science-in-the-making. Although this may seem like a sociological version of cultural analysis that leaves the terms of the debate intact, unlike those who remain committed to conventional postmodern approaches, Latour does not emphasize the vagaries of subjectivism and the relative illusiveness of truth. Such a claim would reiterate Butler's position, namely, that an essential and natural truth is veiled behind Culture's (ultimately failed) attempts to represent or capture it. Instead, Latour effectively redefines "the social" in a more comprehensive way—as a confluence of forces and associations, a collective assembly of human and nonhuman interactions that together produce social facts with referential leverage. In clarifying this notion of a more "realistic realism" that refuses the divide between Nature and Culture, Latour draws on the contributions of actor-network theory (ANT)[11] to explain how this works. Preferring Michel Serres's notion of "quasi-object" rather than "object," Latour explains, "Real quasi-objects do not have the characteristic of being things out there, passive and boring, waiting to be unveiled. Things become active, and the collective becomes made of things—circulating things—which do not have the characteristics they have in the realist argument. So these hybrids (quasi-objects) start resembling what our world is made of. It is not that there are a few hybrids; it is that there are *only* hybrids. . . . [A]ctor-network and quasi-object are exactly the same word" (1993b, 261 and 262).

One of the most important aspects of Latour's intervention is this suggestion that nonhumans must be accommodated within the fabric of society and our understanding of agency and intentionality reconceived accordingly. This means that actors no longer appear as fixed entities for they are like "nodes" that emerge within circulating flows of force—the agential fields of networked intentionality (1993b, 261). As words that evoke the passivity of thingness are the conventional foils against which human intention and activity are discovered, Latour acknowledges that the words he uses to conjure the mix and muddle of this "realistic realism" are imperfect: "Every word is good if it can be used to cross the boundary between people and things. . . . The whole notion of actor-network theory is not a very well packaged argument, but the rule is simple: do not use culture, the content of science, or discourse as the cause of the phenomenon. So the vocabulary of actor-network theory is voluntarily poor. It is not a metalanguage, but an infralanguage. Its core principle is not to limit a priori who or which are the actors and their properties" (1993b, 263).

How this network of "distributed agency" that involves human *and* nonhuman "actants" can actually function and communicate its collective energies is especially fascinating to Latour, who responds by calling for a new philosophy of reference. We might consider the example of forensic investigation mentioned earlier as a good illustration of this network's pragmatic interplay because it has the capacity to produce nodes of reference, or evidence, that *effectively* correspond. Latour underlines that the resulting *dispositif* is not a purely human achievement, and he captures the exquisite mystery of its communicative conversions in the simple question —"How do we pack the world into words?" (1999, 24)

The question's disarming challenge is powerfully evoked in "Circulating Reference: Sampling the Soil in the Amazon Forest" (1999), an essay that conveys the sheer wonder of how empirical field research into the physical densities of biological and geological material can transubstantiate into the sort of representational abstractions that we consult in books. The puzzle of reference that Latour is grappling with must accommodate immutability as well as comparative endurance. As he muses, "If I can manage to grasp this *invariant*, this *je ne sais quoi*, I believe, I will have understood scientific reference" (1999, 36). However, his dilemma is to understand how the staying power of this referent persists despite its constant metamorphosis. Science requires "a reversible route that makes it possible to retrace one's footsteps as needed." From scholarly writings, graphs, and mathematical measurements we can verify someone's findings and repeat their observations in exactly the same place and under the same conditions. Latour describes his colleagues and the different expertise they bring to bear on data in the Amazon forest:

Across the variation of matters/forms, scientists forge a pathway. Reduction, compression, marking, continuity, reversibility, standardization, compatibility with text and numbers. . . . No step—except one—[which concerns the accurate documentation of soil color in this particular study] resembles the one that precedes it, yet in the end, when I read the field report, I am indeed holding in my hands the forest of Boa Vista. A text truly speaks of the world. How can resemblance result from this rarely described series of exotic and miniscule transformations obsessively nested into one another so as to keep something constant? (1999, 61)

We will recall that Latour eschews the postmodern solipsism of cultural constructionism because it concedes no place to Nature at all. Indeed, the difference between Nature and Culture, world and interpretation, is regarded as so enormous that the abyss is unbridgeable. However, in the networks of information noted above Latour discovers negotiable pathways that turn this incommensurable gap into a more manageable series of stepping-stones. Instead of a yawning gulf between Nature and Culture we shuttle across little bridges of translation and transfer—passages of metamorphosis where the communication between matter and form is mutually enabled. Importantly, in Latour's reconception the articulation of the referent is actively produced from both sides (Nature *and* Culture, matter *and* form), and this joint enterprise encourages us to embrace the notion that Nature is articulate, communicative, and in a very real sense—intentional.

Given the postmodern conflation of Culture with language, agency, intention—the creative energies of human subjectivity—it is a welcome intervention that muddles these rigid alignments and forces us to rethink the content of the terms and the more general puzzle of relationality/communication and, indeed, scientific efficacy. But is this what Latour is really encouraging us to do here? Is the identity of matter for example, or the ontology of Nature, something to be pondered and reviewed, or has Latour assumed that what constitutes the stuff of Nature remains essentially different and separate, and that this difference should be *added* to Culture's input? Latour is certainly pressing us to question this frame of reference, but has he inadvertently introduced a limit to his own inquiry?

Before we continue it is important to note that the practice of doing critique involves close encounters with another person's way of thinking, with their intellectual commitments and even the temperament and personal idiosyncrasies that animate their writing style. How we manage the intimacy of these exercises, especially when the aim of our analysis might be to discount that position and take our distance from it, already rehearses this difficult question about identity formation and the implications of relationality. Both Judith Butler and Bruno Latour have specifically acknowledged that one of the most pressing issues in political analysis today, as they perceive it, is the question of critique—how to engage others more generously through interconnection; how to avoid the more murderous maneuvers of dialectical reasoning that negate another's position as wrong in order to affirm our own position as right—as *the* one (and only) position.[12] If we want to address the question of Nature or materiality in a way that does not presume that materiality can be either added to, or subtracted from, something that it isn't (Culture, ideation), then how we identify our own position vis-à-vis another's, how we configure this relationship, will anticipate and rehearse this same difficulty.

Keeping this last consideration at the forefront of what I am trying to do in this discussion, I want to emphasize that I share Butler's conviction that there is "no outside of language." My justification for wanting to *naturalize* language and its productive energies rests on considering how strange this "inside" of language might be. It could be likened to the way physicists negotiate the spatial demarcation of what is inside or outside the universe. Inasmuch as the universe is definitively "comprehensive," an all-inclusive everything, then it can have no edge that marks a limitation to this "everything." What seems outside is therefore another aspect of the inside, an answer that also "explains" why the expansion of the universe is described as an expansion into itself. There are suggestive reconfigurations of how we conceive space in these statements and it is something of this implicate order, this in-habiting, that I am trying to encourage here. For this reason, I am persuaded that by studying the workings of language we are not merely looking at a *model* of the world's "intra-actions" that, by dint of being detached from the world's palpable reality, will inevitably prove mistaken. For it seems quite possible that we may be investigating and witnessing an instantiation of a more general articulation and involvement whose collective expression *we are*. In sum, the provocation I am offering, albeit in sketchy fashion and without the many caveats that its apparent simplicity betrays, might be to interpret "there is no outside of language" as "there is no outside of Nature." What do I forfeit in doing this, and more importantly, what might I gain?

This interpretation recuperates what is axiomatic for Butler's argument, namely, "there is no outside of language"—we are agreed, yet in a way that affirms Latour's conviction that Nature is articulate, that there is no radical disconnection between Nature and Culture, and that agency is a distributed, implicated eco-logy with no central, organizing origin. As the conventional bifurcations and political asymmetries that provoke both thinkers to action are now happily awry, is there a way to suggest that despite our differences we share an uncanny alliance?

To recapitulate, it is clear that Butler is vigilant about the dangers of naturalizing arguments because she is convinced that Nature is *pre*-scriptive. It is quite unthinkable to even suggest that Nature is, already, all of those mutating, complex plasticities that Culture's corrective would animate it with. But what of Latour? Is there a way that Latour could be persuaded to embrace my suggestion as a permutation of his own, especially in light of his stated concerns about the agonistics of critique and the need to forge more intimate modes of engagement? After all, it is Latour who comments, "Critique as a repertoire is over. It has run out of steam entirely, and now the whole question is, "how can we be critical, not by distance but by proximity?" (2004a).

Indeed—how to do it? The inclusiveness of Latour's "assembly of assemblies" sounds promising, and it is powerfully explicated in *We Have Never Been Modern* (1993a): it involves a revamped parliament of distributed utterance where human *and* nonhuman discourse in concert to produce referential meaning. But things get weird once "this everything" of a system's communion, its communication, is naturalized; that is, once you insist that Nature reads, writes, and effectively articulates *itself*. Clearly, "the human" has no privileged position as scribe if Nature is, and always was, a self-recording. And yet we needn't fear, as Latour does, that this admission displaces and disregards the wonder of human history and the veritable din of its discord. If "to naturalize" means that we deny such things, then it is surely time to answer Latour's call for a more exuberant reconsideration of the very nature of Nature.

Latour's struggle to marry the movement and contingency of construction with some workable sense of reality is surely realized in the distributed agency, the *dispositif*, of Nature's manifest literacy. However, Latour's insistence that the reader of the world must remain human completely qualifies the meaning of both distribution and agency. For instance, his exasperated rants against sociobiology, deconstruction, and science fundamentalism, warn us that the "danger" in these approaches is their "mutual ideal" to reach "what has not been built at all by any human hand" (2003, 41). Even assuming this accusation were the case, why is this so reprehensible, and is Latour at this point uncannily Butlerian in defending the world's need for a human amanuensis?

Perhaps we should pause here and remember what is most wild and wonderful in the irreverence of Latour's work. Because it is Latour who evokes the provocation of consubstantiality that invites us to rethink identity's Cartesian framework of separate temporal and spatial coordinates, coordinates that discover individuated identities that preexist their connections; causes that are straightforwardly different, and prior to, the effects they engender; or more straightforwardly, individuals (of whatever sort) that preexist their networked encounter. To allow the implications of consubstantiality to work their mystery is to enter a counterintuitive realm where identities might be conceived as emergent "mutualities"—"collectivities" that are not mere aggregates. Latour helps us here, for in his various clarifications of what he means by "network" and "actor" he explains that nets are inseparable from the act that traces them, and further, that this act of tracing isn't done by an actor external to the network that reveals them. In other words, all "parts" of this network "device" are a sort of synchronous, assemblage/emergence. We are reminded here of Michel Foucault's attempt to reconceptualize the *dispositif* of power as a ubiquitous, involved, and generative force: "Relations of power are not in a position of exteriority with respect to other types of relationships (economic processes, knowledge relationships, sexual relations), but are immanent in the latter; they are the immediate effects of the divisions, inequalities, and disequilibriums which occur in the latter, and conversely they are the internal conditions of these differentiations; relations of power are not in superstructural positions, with merely a role of prohibition or accompaniment; they have a directly productive role, wherever they come into play" (Foucault 1980, 94).

My understanding of this phenomenon is that actants materialize in the distributed agency of this tracing, and if they do not preexist this mediation then they will always be *inherently* hybrid. Latour makes much of this appeal to hybridity, yet the implicated scenography that *evolves* these identities is stripped of all magic if we understand hybridity as a composite of *both* "human" *and* "nonhuman." Latour assists us again, when in a different context he describes his impatience with the complacency that informs this simple notion—"both." The context in this particular case is the way a critical sociology can be downright stupid in its management of metaphysical quandaries. To the question "Is constructed reality constructed or real?" Latour notes the "mildly blasé smile" that greets the answer "both," an answer that shows no appreciation that identity and relationality are questions to be considered and not facts to be assumed. Latour lets fire. "How I despise this little 'both' that obtains so cheaply a veneer of depth that passes nonetheless for the ultimate critical spirit. Never was critique less critical than when accepting as an obvious answer what should be, on the contrary, a source of utter bewilderment" (2003, 35–36).

This reminds us of Latour's provocation mentioned above, "how to be critical by proximity," achieved, perhaps, by making yourself at home in the very logic of your opponent's argument and showing how the direction of that argument can comprehend a very different set of implications. The strategy illustrates the "universe within"—the inherent potential, the open-ended and "intermediating" insinuations that in-form all positions and identities, and trouble their definitive separation and even their inherent constitution. Latour's emphasis on the hybrid nature of identity and his awareness that recourse to a notion of conjunction, or aggregation, is inadequate to this complexity must surely beg the question of how the respective identities of the human *and* nonhuman are defined and kept apart. Why, for example, does Nature require a human scribe to represent itself, to mediate or translate its identity?

When we posit a natural object, a plant for example, we do not need to assume that it is unified and undifferentiated: on the contrary, this one thing is internally divided from itself, a communicating network of cellular mediations and chemical parsings. It is a functioning laboratory, a technological apparatus whose intricate operations are finely elaborated—an "intermediate" node that already articulates its ecological significance in a way that incorporates and blurs the outside with/in the inside. Given this, why is it so difficult to concede that Nature already makes logical alignments that enable it to refer productively to itself, to organize itself so that it can be understood—by itself? If we return to Latour's explanation of circulating reference as a mutual "construction" of human *and* nonhuman in the soil study, it is clear that, for Latour, the soil offers itself as the material origin or object *for* study. Locked in at one end of a continuum, Nature needs to be cultivated, cultured, and coaxed to reveal its secrets. Its lessons are educed by something that, inasmuch as it has the capacity to reveal and encode, cannot be a natural operation by definition. For Latour then, Nature is not itself a laboratory, an experimental, communicative enterprise.

I could conclude the argument by suggesting that Nature does not require human literary skills to write its complexity into comprehensible format. However, if I did this I would actually be reiterating the premise of Latour's position all over again by dividing "human" from "nonhuman": those "non-humans" simply don't need us ... don't be so pompous in assuming that they do! But perhaps there is a position that can affirm the human, *with* Latour, and even with a sociobiological, deconstructive twist that will address Latour's concerns about such "science fundamentalists" and "brain in a vat" naysayers, yet in a way that will allow their work to challenge us and not simply define our perceptiveness against their foolishness.

My suggestion is to try a more counterintuitive gambit, namely, to generalize the assumed capacities of humanness in a way that makes us wonder about their true content; after all, what do we really mean by agency, distributed or otherwise, or by intentionality and literacy? For example, why condemn the sociobiologist E. O. Wilson because he sees humanity reflected in the behavior of ants, in their animal husbandry and finessed horticultural skills, in the political complexities of their caste system, their slaving behaviors, the adaptive ministrations of their nursery regimes, their language, and Culture? Admittedly and importantly, E. O. Wilson looks for the explanatory biological *pre*-scription for social life. But there is a way to reread this work and ventilate its reductionist tendencies. When we explain away this social complexity as an anthropomorphic projection whose comparison diminishes what is specific to human be-ing we automatically secure the difference of our identity *against* the insect (Nature) and reiterate that agrarian cultivation and animal husbandry (Culture) first appeared with Neolithic peoples. We hang on to such assumptions by insisting that natural "smarts," clear evidence of engineering intelligence, social complexity, ciphering skills, and evolutionary innovation, are just programs, the mere expression of instinctual behaviors. It is understandable why both Butler and Latour for that matter would reject the suggestion that human subjectivity, self-consciousness, and agency are "mere" programs. But what is a program if it can rewrite itself? Certainly not *pre-scriptive* in any fixed and immutable sense. Surely, the point is not to take away the complexity that Culture seems to bring to Nature but to radically reconcepetualize Nature "altogether."

The distributed agency of a "human nature" would "act, or communicate, at a distance." This quantum puzzle is actively embraced in "Circulating Reference," where Latour ponders how soil samples taken from the Brazilian savanna can maintain ontological constancy through the variety of instrumental translations, representations, and transformations they undergo—from soil, crumbling between the researcher's fingers, to its final recordings on many sheets of paper. Latour assures us, "Here it is no longer a question of reduction [of the soil into words and graphs] but of transubstantiation" (1999, 64). "Transubstantiation" is a religious term, and yet one that could just as well be applied to quantum phenomena. It certainly evokes an abyssal crossing. However this is not the gulf between Nature and Culture that Butler finds insurmountable; and nor is it the gulf between Nature and Culture across which Latour discovers many little bridges of cooperation. This radical disjunction/inseparability is comprehensive—a fault line that runs throughout all of human nature. It articulates the nonlocal within the local, Nature within Culture, and human within nonhuman. The superposition of these differences means that any identity is articulated with and by all others—consubstantiality and Latour's transubstantiation are one and the same. This is a comprehensive process, a process of comprehension, a material reality.

What happens if Nature is neither lacking nor primordial, but rather, a plenitude of possibilities, a cacophony of convers(at)ion? Indeed, what if it is that same force field of articulation, reinvention, and frisson that we are used to calling—"Culture"? If we embrace the provocations in this suggestion then the conventional landscape of political intervention for those whose identities are denigrated as more primitive (because closer to Nature) shifts considerably. Should feminism and race politics reject the conflation of "woman" or "the other" with "Nature," or instead, take it as an opportunity to consider the question of origins and identity once again?

5. (Con)founding "the Human"

Incestuous Beginnings

Keeping It All Inside

Despite the various and sometimes disparate methodologies and perspectives that jostle together under the umbrella term "critical theory," there is general agreement that the properties and capacities attributed to the humanist subject, or *cogito*, are not all that they seem. Psychoanalytic interpretations of the subject, for example, uncover a fragile figure who is radically incapable of knowing himself; a subject who lacks the ability to remember her past without significantly reinventing it; a subject whose most personal and private desires originate elsewhere. If we accept this and concede that the subject is, indeed, an unreliable witness in the matter of her or his own life,[1] then we are confronted by an extraordinary assault on our conventional assessments of political and ethical accountability: we can no longer rely on appeals to the subject's agency, intention, reason, and sense of responsibility if all these terms are now seriously qualified. The unsettling of humanist precepts is also apparent in discourse theories, as well as in historical and materialist accounts of the subject. There is a shared need to disarticulate the subject as an agential origin and to explain the individual as a product of social and historical forces, discursive formations, and cultural "patternments."[2] In sum, the individual cannot preexist her interpellation into social and discursive meaningfulness if she is "spoken" into being by social and political frames of reference, and only *then* rendered recognizable to others, and to herself.

Things get even more curious when we include within these frames the facts of anatomy, sexual identity, and the specificity of sensual pleasure and sexuality, because even bodily experience will reflect historical and cultural contingencies that translate into perception and sensation. Although at first glance our anatomy and what we do with it may appear as natural facts that we hold in common with all members of our species, both poststructuralist and postmodern representations of the subject, as well as medical and empirical evidence from anthropology and history, suggest that what constitutes pleasure and pain varies dramatically across time and space.[3]

According to these theoretical approaches we are unable to exit particular historical and cultural frames of reference and return to a prior moment before their institution, or even to access some external yet quite different state of life that might be contemporaneous with them. The process of subject formation, which in everyday parlance is the forging of the individual as a "sensible" entity, is said to take place within, indeed, to require, a bounded system of social forces. This boundary, or bar that marks a radical separation between the origin/Nature/the animal and a second-order system of complexity/Culture/the human, secures the difference and distance from that primordial state of being by emphasizing the absolute status of this limit and the complex evolution that has taken place *since* its installation. Whether we pitch our theoretical allegiances with the intellectual tradition that favors hermeneutic circles, Jacques Lacan's bar of prohibition, Fredric Jameson's "prison-house of language," Michel Foucault's "no outside power/knowledge," or perhaps Jacques Derrida's "no outside of text," there is a common attempt in these spatial metaphors to establish a field of productive energy whose changing effects derive from their *internal* relations. Not surprisingly, political activists who are persuaded that things can and should be different have found this epigenetic productivity, this ongoing re-creation of identity and opportunity, immensely attractive. What is important here is that after nearly half a century of such arguments, it now seems to go without saying that this space of contestation and potential promise has been equated with the workings of Culture.[4]

Given this, it is little wonder that cultural critics who are committed to these styles of thinking experience genuine unease when it comes to naturalizing arguments: after all, according to most critical theories, Nature is *pre*scriptive by definition. Nature is the ineffable—that state of primordial life that precedes language and to which direct access is denied. Any sign of Nature, inasmuch as it is a sign, will always/already be a cultural interpretation: in short, Nature as such is absent from the representations of it.

But there are problems here, the most obvious being the surreptitious return to Cartesianism and the conservative legacies that the Nature versus Culture division implies. This recuperation is rarely remarked because the terms of its repetition have changed through a veritable sleight of hand. In what we might call the humanist version of Cartesianism, the difference between Nature and Culture, or body and mind, is perceived as patently apparent, an adjudication that can be tested through reflection. Against this view, an antihumanist Cartesianism that discovers the unconscious *within* the conscious understands reflection as a hall of mirrors that deflects one's capacity to know the difference between a fact and an interpretation—namely, the difference between Nature proper and a representation of it. Despite their differences, which are considerable, both humanist and antihumanist positions regard the identity of the human as self-evident, a cultural artifact of unique complexity: thought and the technology of language are the inalienable capacities of humanness for both sides of this debate. Indeed, even feminist and queer theory, for example, will strive to disengage "otherness" from its associations with Nature so that the recognition and legitimacy afforded the human can be rendered more inclusive.

If finding ways to keep "the in-itself of Nature" out of the play of significance has been a matter of ongoing vigilance, a political practice in itself, more recent shifts in intellectual attentions, coupled with quite dramatic medical and computational breakthroughs in the sciences, threaten to render the defensive reasoning in these positions increasingly irrelevant. After all, how does one explain the referential purchase of forensic investigation, genetic testing, and the like, the predictive capacity of mathematical algorithms in computational programs and so on? As cultural constructs, or models *of* a world that cannot in reality *be* that world, it is entirely unclear how such representational abstractions might be deemed to work at all. This is not to suggest that a critical tradition that discovers all manner of prejudices in the very models of analysis has been misguided, or that scientific results are not contestable. Surely the more interesting point is to consider how cultural criticism and scientific insights can *both* hold true: the value of one is not necessarily secured by proving the error of another, any more than the determination of an error will simply erase its productive and even insightful effects.

Coupled with this question about the pragmatic purchase of scientific reference—the question of Nature at its most insistent—is the sobering

evidence that the textualizing of the subject and the object in the humanities is increasingly underscored in scientific methodologies and their outcomes. From the study of astronomical bodies and their "signatures" to the
operations of the tiniest signs of life, the world appears as a body of interlocking information. The fascinating provocation that presents itself here
is that these interwoven, interacting sign systems that articulate the most
intricate and intimate complexities are not just languages that are trans-
ferred between computers, people, atoms, or cells. In other words, these
languages are not alien technologies that are acquired and exchanged between preexisting entities—between senders and receivers who communicate with each other. What is most challenging in this global field of
information is that if the material being of these senders and receivers is
also information, then the autonomy of each of these communication
"nodes" is compromised. This sense that there is no outside the textile of
information begs the question of how an identity, of whatever sort, is
individuated from the process of its emergence and ongoing reproduction
and maintenance.

What are we to make of the ubiquity of these textual involvements and
their manifestation across all modes of knowledge, all expressions of being? Is this inversion of inside with/in outside (the humanities with the
sciences, Culture with Nature, the ideation and abstraction of language
with the manifest substance of physical reality) yet more evidence that we
remain on the inside of metaphysics and epistemology, an arena whose
operations define human identity and its unique ability to read, to write, to
think? Or have all these terms assumed such curious dimensions that we
might even consider that Nature as such might *be* a meta-physics, an
involved meditation, mediation, and reproduction of itself that is essentially queer in character?

As the relevance of explanatory models that attribute Culture with primary and causal force is still very much alive, what I want to do here is to
follow my own advice and try to reform the terms of reference that are
routine in these approaches. My aim is to acknowledge the importance of
cultural interventions that explain the problematic nature of identity and
the perverse and hybrid forms of communication/intercourse that produce them. However, I want to argue that we do not need to circumscribe
the arena of production and reproduction by segregating what is properly
cultural from what is then, and inevitably, deemed alien, primordial, and

inarticulate. What I propose is not a simple reiteration of the sort of cultural constructionist arguments that remind us that what *appears* as Nature is better understood as the dissembling of Culture; or its corollary, that intervention and contestation are necessarily cultural and social endeavors. Nor am I interested in resolving the question by reverting to the logic of assemblage, Nature *and* Culture. Instead, I will at least try to suggest why the strange condensations that confuse and collapse differences into the mirror-maze of an "always/already" might better be described as facts of Nature.

The Queer Entanglements of Being Human

The suggestion that what has become axiomatic for cultural constructionist arguments, even the most sophisticated among them, might be inadequate to explain empirical complexity has recently been conceded by Judith Butler. Butler is well known for privileging cultural systems of significance whose mediation and displacement of what, for convenience, we might risk calling "Nature proper," confines it to a shadowy, inaccessible, and therefore unrepresentable existence, albeit one we are compelled, over and over again, to try to represent. Given the increasingly awkward ramifications of this exclusion, Butler's admission is especially timely, as it recognizes that the historical necessity for such interpretive strategies may now be over. As she muses, "I think perhaps mainly in *Gender Trouble* I overemphasize the priority of culture over nature. . . . At the time of *Gender Trouble*, now sixteen years ago, it seemed to me that there was a cultural use of 'natural' arguments to provide legitimacy for natural genders or natural heterosexuality. But that criticism did not take account of a nature that might be, as it were, beyond the nature/culture divide, one that is not immediately harnessed for the aims of certain kinds of cultural legitimation practices" (Butler in Kirby 2006, 144–45). Citing the efforts of the biologist Anne Fausto-Sterling to illustrate a more even-handed approach to the problem, Butler finds in the interactivity of this approach an acknowledgment of the productive contributions that are generated from both sides of the divide. Butler explains the twofold value of Fausto-Sterling's perspective, namely, that "a) biology conditions cultural life and contributes to its forms, and b) cultural life enters into the reproduction of our bodies at a biological level."

Butler derives a sense of affirmation from these words. As she notes, "My sense is that [Fausto-Sterling's] formulation is resonant with my brief effort [in *Bodies That Matter*] to establish a kind of chiasmic relation between the two. After all, she also eschews forms of determinism, either cultural or biological, and yet refuses the collapse of the categories into one another" (Butler in Kirby 2006, 145).

We need to pause and take stock of what is being claimed here, as it will provide a point of departure for the rest of the argument and, hopefully, help to anchor and explain its inevitable confusions. First, it seems fair to say that Butler assumes that Nature and Culture constitute two different entities, or systems of operation. Indeed, despite what Butler will concede as their interactivity, a chiasm "between the two,"[5] it is Fausto-Sterling's refusal to collapse Culture and biology into one another that earns her approval. In sum, whereas Butler previously insisted that analytical discussion was confined to the realm of the cultural, even when it claimed to allow Nature to speak for itself, she is now willing to grant that, inasmuch as these distinct modes of operation do manage some form of intercourse, this fact, and how we talk about it, needs to be revisited. I use the word "intercourse" deliberately here because however we try to "conceive" this interactive interface, this coming together, this copulating necessity that enables human being, it is nourished by our prejudices about the nature of sex, reproduction, sexuality, and sexual difference. Importantly, an appreciation that "natural facts" are always informed by cultural bias is one of the most important contributions that scholars such as Butler have made, and any return to the question of Nature will need to accommodate or reconfigure such insights rather than put them aside. To this end, what follows is not so much a negative critique of Butler's position, an attempt to overturn and dismiss its relevance. On the contrary, it is an endeavor to find a different perspective that respects Butler's political concerns and theoretical commitments, while acknowledging, as she does, that a shift in how we appreciate Nature is now required.

In the scenario described above we are presented with two quite different entities—Nature and Culture. Although each is able to affect and transform the other (chiasmically), their respective identities appear to be given *before* the interactions that affect them. For example, the very assumption that whatever Culture is, it was temporally preceded by something that was not Culture, subtends this logic. And yet the belief in identity as something coherent and wholesome before its intercourse with "otherness," its violation by "otherness," is routinely contested in feminist and queer analysis. Given this, are we right to be suspicious of the repetition of this logic in this instance?

If we retain some sensitivity to the political metaphorics of sexual intercourse, then a second point emerges. Butler inadvertently installs a sort of incest taboo, a moral bar of prohibition about what will count as intercourse as well as what forms it can take, when she conflates cultural activity with political activity, and political activity with the desire to prohibit, restrict, and dominate. As we see in the first quotation, the apparently benign nature that Fausto-Sterling's work investigates is rendered an acceptable force of transformation that we can *safely* include in our analyses because it is beyond (or before) the desire to use, to harness, to legitimate, and to calculate. The evocation of this prelapsarian view of Nature, which in other contexts Butler would be the first to criticize, inevitably leads her to attribute intent and calculation to Culture—the fall from benign intent, or perhaps more accurately, the fall that the arrival of intent forecasts! It seems that Fausto-Sterling's Nature is incapable of mirroring, and certainly incapable of actually being, the agential processes, the manipulations, and political calculations that we conventionally define as Culture.

This is not to suggest that these two systems are simply independent of each other. Myriad arguments, indeed, probably most, are happy to acknowledge human indebtedness or dependence *on* Nature—even Descartes conceded this. But what stops us from at least considering that humans are inherently natural, and not in the sense of an aggregation of one part Nature to one part Culture? What would happen if, as Butler fears, these two realms actually did collapse into one? What do we forfeit if we concede that Nature reads and writes, calculates and copulates with itself in the most perverse, creative, and also destructive ways? What if it is political through and through, and this very discussion, here, in this book, is a manifestation of natural intent?[6] If we are to open the question of identity and sexuality more thoroughly, we will need to risk the identity of humanness itself and the logic that operates to indemnify this identity against an outside that appears alien to it, an identity that for too long has pretended not to engage in modes of intercourse that are considered improper, unspeakable—unnatural.

The task I have set myself is to try to evoke the stickier aspects of identity formation, the gender discriminations that are articulated through the Nature/Culture division, and the consonance of this problematic with the puzzle of relationality, intercourse, and reproduction more generally. But where to start? Cultural criticism has made a point of interrogating "initial conditions"—those inherited logics and assumptions that authenticate certain behaviors and ways of being while denigrating others as perverse and improper. However, if we move to the physical sciences and a very different field of inquiry such as quantum relations, we are confronted with an argument that finds "initial conditions" within "final conditions," and signs of what comes second in what must logically come first. Consistent with this spacetime condensation, the difference between concepts (ideality) and material reality (physical objects) seems to collapse, or at least to go awry in some way that no longer makes sense.

Butler's argument in *Bodies That Matter* appears to evoke something similar, inasmuch as ideations are able to "realize," or "materialize," a world. However, the result is not *one* world but, rather, a cultural frame of valuations and normative ideals *through which* bodies are controlled and regulated, albeit imperfectly (1993, 1–2). In other words, Culture enlists Nature into service, but Nature's difference from Culture guarantees its recalcitrance and Culture's ultimate failure to render Nature compliant. Karen Barad describes such approaches with an impatience that reflects my own: "The ubiquitous puns on 'matter' do not, alas, mark a rethinking of the key concepts (materiality and signification) and the relationship between them. Rather, they seem to be symptomatic of the extent to which matters of 'fact' (so to speak) have been replaced with matters of signification (no scare quotes here). Language matters. Discourse matters. Culture matters. There is an important sense in which the only thing that doesn't seem to matter anymore is matter" (2007, 132).

If we take on board the counterintuitive implications, the substantive reality of quantum relations, we become aware that Butler's notion of performative iteration relies uncritically on temporal and spatial separation. For Butler, performativity rests on a foundational difference between Nature and Culture: the failure of fit between Culture's attempts to naturalize norms, or to render the body compliant, becomes the motor of representation and change.[7] However, the description of entities as either separate to each other *or* inseparable, even when interpenetrating (as Butler's term "chiasmic" concedes) is inadequate to the complexity of quantum entanglement. Similarly, the temporal differences that separate past, present, and future into discrete "events" appear strangely synchronous in quantum accounts, where thought experiments can anticipate what will have already taken place—the evocation of a deconstructive muddle is strangely apt. Remarkably, such assertions are no longer considered mere thought experiments to be entertained by scientific boffins. As noted in the previous chapter, the results of these experiments have been retrospectively actualized and empirically verified.[8]

The Incestuous Nature of Initial Conditions
Rethinking the Familiar, the Self-Same

Let us return the discussion to the familiar zone of cultural analysis, bearing in mind that by "keeping it all inside" we might well be working with something whose incestuous outcomes are considerably more perverse and involved than the conventions of cultural constructionism, in all its forms, can currently sanction. What we will need to consider is if this shift that discovers cultural or interpretive arguments inside what presents itself as a first-order system (Nature) is an anthropocentric projection, an inevitable representation of cultural and political significance in the guise of natural qualities and capacities. This is Butler's position, namely, that because Nature will always appear as a sign (to be read), and inasmuch as Nature isn't literate and a sign is therefore a cultural artifact, then what we take to be Nature is really Culture (in disguise). Perhaps ironically, given what I am about to argue, the strength of Butler's position has, to my mind, always been her commitment to the internal workings of *one* system. Until recently, she did not sacrifice the intellectual rigor that attended this commitment and its difficulties for the complacent solution of addition—Nature *and* Culture—although her latest concession to biological explanation marks the end of this strategy. Consistent with this analysis of how difference and heterogeneity might arise from *within* a system's internal workings, I want to keep faith with Butler's earlier focus on just one system. However, whereas Butler draws analytical leverage from the term "Culture," I want to include all that Butler evokes under this banner, yet insist that a more accurate term for this unified, if heterogeneous, field of expression is "Nature." As we will see, there will be no need to position biological explanations outside this system and then wonder how Nature and Culture, chiasmically or otherwise, "get together."

Clearly, my strategy does not conform to Butler's stated warnings about the best way to manage Nature as we concede a place for it in our discussions. Recall that Fausto-Sterling was commended because she "eschews forms of determinism, either cultural or biological, and yet refuses the collapse of the categories into one another." Against this, I will argue that it is only by committing these perceived misdemeanors that the most mind-twisting and challenging implications of the Nature question can actually emerge. Admittedly, if the identity of "the human" cannot be defined against Nature to secure its difference, then things will get decidedly strange. What happens to truth, to scientific reference (for this is the most enduring puzzle that discussions about Nature must address), if it is in the nature of Nature to be political, perverse, contestatory—and to mutate accordingly?[9]

A good place to begin this reconsideration, especially as its conceptual geography will be more familiar to a humanities audience, is Judith Butler's exploration of biological reference as it informs sexual identity and sexuality.[10] However, before we begin, I need to explain why a text that addresses the vagaries of the signifier (Culture) might be an appropriate place to discover the complexity of Nature, a complexity that requires no supplement. I can certainly anticipate why my imagined reader might expect the assault on cultural constructionism to arrive from elsewhere, for example, from the physical and biological sciences. While such strategies are perfectly valid, the special signature of my own mode of inquiry, given its commitment to originary entanglement, is something more ironic: I want to suggest that arguments intended to exemplify Culture proper as a contained and separate system have much to say about the impossibility of such a claim.

In "The Lesbian Phallus and the Morphological Imaginary," Butler (1993) ponders the puzzle of anatomy and opens with a detailed reference to Freud's essay, "On Narcissism: An Introduction," where the analyst dilates on the nature of the libido. According to Freud, the libido has a fluid and quantitative dimension, and it is through the accrual and diminution of its "love energy" that the personal significance of bodily experience is registered, or felt. The movement of these excitations is likened to an economy because its forces are cathected, or invested, through fluctuating intensities across the body, as well as outwardly, into the bodies of others. Evidence of this fluctuation can be seen in the response to pain and injury.

When we think of pain we think of the body's unmediated and most urgent reality, and yet the experience of pain shows radical variation across different cultural and social contexts, as well as marked shifts within the individual subject.[11] A toothache, for example, involves pain that is physically *and* psychically induced, and registered accordingly. And yet the need to use a conjunction in this simple description of hybrid causes tends to install biology as the first, or original cause, whose effects may be modulated by cultural and subjective influence. However, the logic of this temporal two-step that separates Nature from Culture is increasingly confused as Freud extrapolates from the experience of toothache to other examples of libidinal self-investment, including hypochondria. In the latter instance of imaginary physical ailments, the explanatory direction from biological causes to their subjective interpretation is reversed: here, pain arises from psychical forces that manifest as biological symptoms. Noting the "theoretical indissolubility of physical and imaginary injury" in Freud's argument, Butler makes two interesting observations. "This position has consequences for determining what constitutes a body part at all, and, as we shall see, what constitutes an erotogenic body part in particular. In the essay on narcissism, hypochondria lavishes libido on a body part, but in a significant sense, that body part does not exist for consciousness prior to that investiture; indeed, that body part is delineated and becomes knowable for Freud only on the condition of that investiture" (1993, 58).

Anticipating Lacan's argument in "The Mirror Stage," Freud believed that a sense of self was acquired through the realization of body boundaries as the child underwent a developmental separation from the (m)other. And yet the suggestion that self-discovery is provoked by the conscious experience of physical excitation or pain presents us with something of a quandary. How can consciousness be a derivative of corporeal self-discovery if it is already present at its initiation? Butler notes that "it is fundamentally unclear, even undecidable, whether this is a consciousness that imputes pain to the object, thereby delineating it—as is the case in hypochondria— or whether it is a pain caused by organic disease which is retrospectively registered by an attending consciousness" (1993, 59). In this account, self-perception is not attributed to biological causes alone (assuming there could be such a thing), but to an erotogenicity that renders the *idea* of a particular body part coincident with the phenomenology of its perception.

The relevance of this point for the broader argument is simply stated.

Whereas we might readily agree that notions, beliefs, and ideas can be real-ized, or made physically manifest, we rarely consider *how*. I want to suggest that what sits behind this question's prohibition is the possibility that the physical body—biology—conceives itself differently through myriad im-ages, ideas, and notions, such that an idea *is* a biological cause/effect. In other words, "initial conditions" are inherently unstable and mutable, and consciousness cannot be separated out from this biological complexity.

Exploring this question of what comes first, Freud underlines the sexual nature of libidinal self-attention when he suggests that, "the familiar pro-totype [*Vorbild*] of an organ sensitive to pain, in some way changed and yet not diseased in the ordinary sense, is that of the genital organ in a state of excitation" (Freud quoted in Butler 1993, 59). Butler remarks on the at-tribution of masculinity in Freud's use of the definite article, *the* genital organ, yet any sexual specificity vanishes when we realize that other erog-enous zones can substitute for the genitals and respond similarly. The redistribution of libidinal investment from one body part to another means that while the genitals are prototypical of this variable process they do not inaugurate this chain of substitutions. As Freud explains, "We can decide to regard erotogenicity as a general characteristic of all organs and may then speak of an increase or decrease of it in a particular part of the body" (quoted in Butler 1993, 61).

The ambiguity in Freud's clarification provides Butler with a degree of critical purchase, because if male genitals retain no ontological privilege or priority in fact or in symbolic value, then there is more going on than the simple displacement of an original phallic (masculine) privilege and the transference of its erotogenicity to other body parts. Indeed, what can it mean to talk of "*its* erotogenicity," as if the phallus is one single organ, a penis? As Butler describes it, "To be a property of all organs is to be a property necessary to *no* organ, a property defined by its very *plasticity*, *transferability*, and *expropriability*" (1993, 61). And if the properties and capacities of a body part are truly contingent, acquiring recognition *as a result* of libidinal investiture, then "the phallus" is a term for the *process* of investiture—for the action of delineating, identifying, and eroticizing. It follows from this that the identity and integrity of any one organ will always be compromised because its "singling out" is a relational discrimination whose construal involves, and retains, its context. Butler's explanation of what is going on in Freud's example of the toothache, that "jaw-tooth's aching hole," provides a wonderful illustration of this congested and condensed network of referral, "a punctured instrument of penetration, an inverted vagina dentata, anus, mouth, orifice in general, the spectre of the penetrating instrument penetrated." Even the tooth's identity is ambivalent, appearing as "that which bites, cuts, breaks through, and enters," but also, "that which is itself already entered, broken into" (Butler 1993, 61).

But why should libidinal transfer be described in terms of paternity? Through a sliding metonymy of references that presumes the identities it is trying to explain, Freud conflates the generative power of the phallus with the male organ. As we have seen, the phallus is more accurately understood as a productive *process* of delineation through which entities/body parts emerge into identifiable significance. When this transformative dynamism is arrested and likened to a thing-like property however, man appears to *have* the phallus, just as woman appears to *be* this erotic and valued object.

With such considerations in mind, we can appreciate why Butler's reflections on the lesbian phallus are provocative. Is it really a failed copy of a male original, a substitute for woman's bodily lack and its corollary—the sexual incapacity of the lesbian? Freud's own conviction about the nature of libidinal energy thwarts an explanatory return to a single origin because the libido is a *field* of energy whose uneven distribution throughout the body motors the infant's self-discovery. Of course, the notion of "self" in this description is somewhat premature because the infant's self-recognition as a bounded individual among many has yet to take place: prior to this, the plenum of the world is *self-same* with the child.[12]

And here we need another qualification and one we will have good reason to return to, for the infant's apparent coincidence with the world need not imply an homogenized unity, or undifferentiated plenitude *before* the cut of difference (Culture/language/individuation). It is important to appreciate that this originary "self-same" is a congested and entangled scene of noncoincidence and referral. In other words, the differentiation that the infant perceives remains overwhelming because its complexity has yet to be "properly" interpreted and apportioned a meaningful place. Because Freud sees the infant as inherently fragmented at first, and therefore fractured and certainly "multiple" in what might be described as its primordial identifications, attachments, and desirings (because the other is [also] itself), Freud described human sexuality as constitutionally *bisexual* and *polymorphously perverse.* Although Freud does not provide an exact explanation of bisexuality and questions its meaning and implications throughout his life, it is clear that the difference between masculine and feminine, or male and female, is so muddled by the notion that the binary coordinates of sexual difference cannot explain the term.[13] For this reason, rather than think of bisexuality in ways that already presume identity (for example, male plus female), it might be more useful (and theoretically rigorous) to consider bisexuality as the splitting of desire that renders all identity incoherent and perverse *from the start*: deprived of a single origin, a unified identity, intention, or goal, the teleological notion of sexuality that segregates bodies and pleasures into distinct identities and appropriate practices has no fixed and stable foundation.

It follows from this that the attribution of the libido's origin to the male organ and the inevitable valorization of the penis as *the* generative site (the phallus) is an imaginary illusion that can only be sustained if the trans-genesis of libidinal energy is denied and repressed. And yet, although this denial naturalizes privilege, the very nature of its deceptive manufacture will remain a structural flaw in its maintenance—something Butler considers "the promising spectre of its destabilization" (1993, 63). The system's fragility is again underlined when Freud describes erotogenic discovery and self-preoccupation in terms of illness, pain, and suffering. As we saw earlier in the example of hypochondria, a case of narcissistic self-absorption, the subject's fascination is expressed by delineating a particular body part as inherently fragile, sick, and in need. By making the theatrical performance of illness exemplary in the eroticization of the body—"a libidinal projection of the body-surface which in turn establishes its epistemological accessibility" (1993, 63)—Freud underlined the social fabrication of sexuality and its potential concatenation with illness.

In "The Ego and the Id" Freud draws an even closer link between sexuality and illness when he finds that the hypochondriac's self-preoccupation is, as Butler describes it, "symptomatic of the structuring presence of a moralistic framework of guilt" (1993, 63). According to Freud, guilt arises because the internal dynamic of narcissistic self-possession must be externalized toward objects and other subjects if we are to experience a normal sexuality. To refuse this social demand by reinvesting in the self is to take a guilty pleasure, and yet this pleasure is fraught with ambivalence: on the one hand, its unsanctioned satisfaction exacts physical illness and suffering, but on the other, if the resulting illness effectively deceives society then the underlying narcissism is affirmed. Can the difference between pleasure and pain be decided in this example?

Aware of the ambiguous possibilities that attend an "eroticized hypochondria," Butler notes that if conformity to regulatory sexual ideals requires prohibition and the threat of pain, then the failure of these interdictions, or their qualified success, must induce irregular outcomes: "They may delineate body surfaces that do not signify conventional heterosexual polarities. These variable body surfaces or bodily egos may thus become sites of transfer for properties that no longer belong properly to any anatomy" (1993, 64).

The possibility of the lesbian phallus makes its appearance at this juncture, and the question of anatomy *as such* assumes special pertinence. However, before returning to this provocative proposition we should underline that the link that connects sickness with narcissism, the love of self, is something Freud associates with homosexuality, the love of self-same. What is purported to be an inwardly directed, primitive, and presocial libidinal energy must be turned around in a heterosexual economy and aimed toward others. Freud argued that the successful taking on of these heteronormative requirements coincides with the development of a conscience—the will to conform to social regulation. Thus, if the propriety of sexual identity depends on "the introjection of the homosexual cathexis" (Butler 1993, 65), then the effective maintenance of normality is built on the pain and guilt that now attaches to this unsanctioned and prohibited pleasure.

However, Butler suggests that the pain of self-beratement and denial does more than simply abandon a love object, for something "productive" is also at work as the psyche organizes the body into an imaginary schema of meaningful parts. If the body *appears* in the form that it does because it is a living history of felt significance, then the social prohibition against certain love objects will reform those libidinal investments to preserve and memorialize them:

> If, then, as Freud contends, pain has a delineating effect, i.e., may be one way in which we come to have an idea of our body at all, it may also be that gender-instituting prohibitions work through suffusing the body with a pain that culminates in the projection of a surface, that is, a sexed morphology which is at once a compensatory fantasy and a fetishistic mask. And if one must either love or fall ill, then perhaps the sexuality

that appears as illness is the insidious effect of such a censoring love. Can the very production of the *morphe* be read as an allegory of prohibited love, the *incorporation* of loss? (1993, 65)

Butler's argument moves from Freud's meditation on narcissism to Jacques Lacan's reformulation of Freud's theory in "The Mirror Stage" and "The Signification of the Phallus." Lacan will argue that the child's apperception of itself as a coherent and bounded entity in space means that it must learn to identify itself from another's perspective, that is, from an external vantage point that it cannot occupy. Using the child's recognition of itself in a mirror as an analogy for this more general process of speculation, Lacan attributes the resulting morphology, or bodily outline that the child assumes, to a dynamic vacillation between projection and misrecognition. Several things are important here. First, the disjunction between the infant's perception of its amorphous ubiquity, an "all over the place" that Lacan punningly describes as an "hommelette," and the specular idealization of itself as a coherent (other) entity with control and agency will never be resolved. This means that the ego is, and will remain, a *bodily* ego, whose identity is not so much a fixed property as it is an ongoing dynamic of *re*-cognition and mutation. And second, Lacan will also argue that the morphological schema that inaugurates the ego is also the threshold of the visible world. In other words, how we perceive the difference between people, objects, and their interrelationships (the shape and definition of otherness) will be extruded through a corporeal imaginary that has constitutive force: the subject *is* this process, where the differentiation of world and ego emerge in the same reflex/reflection. Butler summarizes: "As imaginary, the ego as object is neither interior nor exterior to the subject, but the permanently unstable site where that spatialized distinction is perpetually negotiated; it is this ambiguity that marks the ego as *imago*, that is, as an identificatory relation. Hence, identifications are never simply or definitively *made or achieved*; they are insistently constituted, contested, and negotiated (1993, 76).

Butler certainly agrees with Lacan that the child's bodily ego is peopled with others, inasmuch as its very anatomy is informed with social relations and their dynamic conversions. Indeed, the possibility of a lesbian phallus will depend on the psychosocial open-endedness of the body's perceived anatomy. However, Butler finds something disturbing in the way Lacan's argument seems to have it both ways. Lacan explains the organizational logic of the Symbolic order, those cultural and linguistic structures into which the child is interpellated, as a *given* system of binary identifications whose positions are determined by a transcendental signifier—the phallus. Despite this, he also insists that the Symbolic order exceeds *specific* cultural or social ascriptions because it operates as the universal principle of differentiation that motors all languages. It is for this reason that Lacan will echo Freud by insisting that the phallus should not be confused with the penis, or indeed, with any organ or particular imaginary effect. But what can be done if we accept this thesis? As Butler's critical energies are focused on the need to contest political inequities, her concern is that Lacan's "explanation" has the performative consequence of investing the penis (and masculinity) with the symbolic privilege accorded the phallus, and in a way that places the male organ's political significance beyond question.

Through a close reading of the twists and turns in Lacan's argument, Butler uses the analyst's own position to question the distinction he makes between the Symbolic order and the Imaginary, that wishful process of representational identification that enables the infant to overcome (and deny) its inadequacies. Although the logic for the division that Butler contests is inadvertently recuperated in her presumption that cultural forces must be quite different from natural ones, we can nevertheless extrapolate from her deconstruction of the different systems in Lacan's argument to acknowledge what we might describe as "the constant instability" of biology.

With Butler as our guide, we are reminded that for any body part to be delineated as identifiable and separate, the body's overall erotogenicity and signifiability will be involved, indeed, the body part will emerge from a process that incorporates the whole of the body in the "part's" transvaluation. Lacan would surely agree in principle that the phallus can take myriad imaginary forms other than the penis, including objects. However, when Butler takes Lacan at his word and raises the gender-troubling specter of a lesbian phallus, the political investments that align phallic mastery with "the mutually exclusive trajectories of castration anxiety and penis envy" (1993, 84–5) are no longer straightforward. Without recourse to a stable point of origin that can anchor the vagaries of the bodily ego as well as its dispositions of desire, all identity, including sexual identity as well as that of a body part, are rendered ambiguous. Lacan's work would certainly concede this point, or even underline it. Nevertheless, Butler perceives something more subversive in the "contradictory formulation" of a lesbian phallus that "crosses the orders of *having* and *being*":

> If men are said to "have" the phallus symbolically, their anatomy is also a site marked by having lost it; the anatomical part is never commensurable with the phallus itself. In this sense, men might be understood to be both castrated (already) and driven by penis envy (more properly understood as phallus envy). Conversely, in so far as women might be said to "have" the phallus and fear its loss (and there is no reason why that could not be true in both lesbian and heterosexual exchange, raising the question of an implicit heterosexuality in the former, and homosexuality in the latter), they may be driven by castration anxiety. (1993, 85)

If the bodily ego *necessarily* incorporates such phantasmatic cross-overs, then normative bifurcations of sexual identity and desire must involve a failure of fit, which is borne, or made legible, by "marginal" subjectivities even though this failure pertains to everyone. Importantly, Butler rejects the idea that the so-called margin is constitutively different from the center, an insight that complicates a pluralist politics of inclusion, as well as its inverse—the privileging of the margin as a site of play and possibility outside the repressive structures of heteronormative identity. Instead, what is emphasized in Butler's argument is that structures of subject formation have no central point of authorization, no overarching logic of noncontradiction that separates heteronormative forms of exchange from those that seem so different. If structures of identification are so thoroughly messy, implicated, and ambiguous for all of us that the difference between who has the phallus and who is the phallus is a social and political determination that cannot be anatomically decided, then the seeming invariance of phallic reference is a performative fiction.

As we have seen, Butler focuses on the Lacanian thesis that the phallus inaugurates the signifying chain and sets it into motion because it is radically incommensurate with its representational substitutions. Lacan's thesis is certainly a provocative proposition because the givenness of an origin and an entity are replaced by process and irresolution—a dynamism in which the lived significance of anatomy is in play and the absolute invariance of reference is undone. This is the leverage point where Butler locates her question about the conflation of the penis with the privileged signifier of the phallus. If "the phallus symbolizes only through taking anatomy as its occasion, then the more various and unanticipated the anatomical (and non-anatomical) occasions for its symbolization, the more unstable that signifier becomes" (1993, 90). Consequently, if the lesbian can have and be the phallus at the same time (as Lacan's separation of the phallus from the penis must imply), then the facticity of the body and related notions about what a body can and cannot do are subjected to "an aggressive reterritorialization" (1993, 86). In other words and ironically, the implications of a lesbian phallus acknowledge the complex dimensions and sensate reality of *everyone's* phantasmatic anatomy, as well as the myriad objects and expressions that desire can assume.

What has been established so far is that Butler's work rests on a vigilant interrogation of the coherence and purity of identity, especially the presumption that identity is there from the start. Consequently, an important platform in her critical strategy has been to return to anatomy in order to reconceive its referential stability. In sum then, Butler has argued that an individual's body boundary (the imago, or phantasmatic body) is an erotic surface whose individual perception is forged from social relations that are always evolving and shifting the body's contours and desires. In other words, the delineation of this imaginary anatomy is borne from the pain of loss, and it remains a fragile and unstable "edifice" for just this reason. Forged from failure and incapacity, it is unable to re-present an ideal it cannot have and cannot be: it is a misrecognition of itself, a "dissimulated effect," "a fetishistic mask," "a compensatory fantasy" of grieving melancholia for what is now prohibited (1993, 65).

Consistent with this rather forlorn scene of unrequited desire whose reproductive effects are generated from the incommensurability, or prohibited intercourse, between a now inaccessible (forbidden) Nature and Culture, we will recall that Butler seizes on the erotics of hypochondria, the ability of pain to rewrite loss as pleasure, to exemplify this general process of transvaluation: it delineates body parts, ailments, and objects as erotic memorials to a maternal loss that exceeds representation. The ability of the body to be something other than it seems, to incorporate the alien as itself, explains why Butler describes masculine, heterosexual melancholy as a "refusal to grieve the masculine as a possibility of love; [just as] a feminine gender is formed (taken on, assumed) through the incorporative fantasy by which the feminine is excluded as a possible object of love, an exclusion never grieved, but 'preserved' through the heightening of feminine identification itself" (1993, 235). The uncanny manifestations of prohibition are further underlined in the comment, "In this sense, the 'truest' lesbian melancholic is the strictly straight woman, and the 'truest' gay male melancholic is the strictly straight man" (Butler 1993, 235).

It is politically significant to appreciate, as we do in these transfigurative examples, that prohibition is never purely negative. However, the insistence that anatomy's inherent mutability should be understood as illusion, or fiction, deserves further attention. Although things are certainly not as they seem in Butler's account, her critique of identity and anatomical facticity remains tethered to their unproblematic status as foundation. Instead of the bisexual perversion that renders sexual identity improper and undecidable *from the start, and forever after*, Butler's analysis effectively untangles the ambiguity to reveal a truth behind the counterfeit, as we see in the following example of maternal identity. If we are to understand female identity and femininity as essential and uncontroversial attributes that define the mother, then the masquerade of identity-forming reversals that her (supposed) loss engenders makes sense. But surely this is far from the case. The mother is deemed a phallic mother because s/he lacks nothing. S/he is the (w)hole, the world, the parenting plenitude of transfiguration and genesis that, at one and the same time, expresses the child's "own" difference from itself; the constitutive difference that drives the child's desire for itself/another. In this scene of morphogenesis where identity is never established once and for all, the m/other is a ubiquitous figure. And if s/he is never simply lost or absent, then what is the status of the term "misrecognition" that founds Lacan's thesis, as well as the masquerading ruse, the presumption of illusion and fiction, that underpins Butler's description of the "truest lesbian" and the "truest straight man"? Butler's refusal to accede to the incestuous nature of Nature, its "unnatural" capacity to reproduce itself in myriad manifestations that, in a very real sense, are all true, is in evidence here.

But do we gain a better sense of the complex operations of identity formation if we consider that this involved complicity is not reducible to duplicity—Culture's misrecognition of what is actually (naturally?) true? This is a difficult and elusive point that requires careful exegesis. We will recall, for example, that Freud interprets the hypochondriac's sickness as a foil for narcissistic self-attention, a foil whose pleasurable suffering incorporates the guilt that attends the production of a body that will not conform to the demands society makes of it. The narrative resolution of what to do with this initial prepossession that is defined *against* society is to hide "it." Why, however, should we assume that the plenitude of primordial erotogenicity (prepossession) is an individuated "something" that is radically separate from an outside when child and world, or what we retrospectively bifurcate into these identifying differences (internal and external, self and other), are originally consubstantial?[14] "Consubstantial" in this sense evokes the "sameness" of an identity that endures (invariance) through morphogenesis (variation). This is the real puzzle, a veritable brain twister, and its dimensions defy the sort of explanatory "resolution" of the paradox in Butler's reversal. The very notions of sameness and difference, homo and hetero, natural and cultural, are not just implicated—a notion that presumes their segregation before they are compromised, or chiasmically involved. If identity is *never given*, and the entanglement of these terms of reference can never be segregated, then the constitutive paradox of identity becomes strange indeed.

Why is so much at stake in the subtleties of this muddled involvement, and why should we be concerned? Butler's own argument helps us here, for she repeatedly questions the commonality, the sense of sameness that subtends the description of the *homo*sexual, and even judges the existence of a lesbian sexuality "an impossible monolith" (1993, 85). The developmental narrative that discovers a primordial, narcissistic self-possession at the origin, and *naturally* equates this with the love of self-same (homoeroticism), will quite logically presume that social maturity and the acquisition of a conscience are more evolved achievements—the proper attributes of the heterosexual who is male. Butler alerts us to the danger in this logic, as we see in this cautionary note: "The pathologization of erotogenic parts in Freud calls to be read as a discourse produced in guilt, and although the imaginary and projective possibilities of hypochondria are useful, they call to be dissociated from the metaphorics of illness that pervade the description of sexuality. This is especially urgent now that the pathologization of sexuality generally, and the specific description of homosexuality as the paradigm for the pathological as such, are symptomatic of homophobic discourse on AIDS" (1993, 64).

Quite clearly, the violence of homophobia cannot be attenuated by such moral appeals if the logic that discriminates homosexual from heterosexual identity remains intact. Homophobia, misogyny, and racism are nourished by the notion that a primitive hypersexualized self-absorption pre-cedes the social, and this original incapacity is defined against social order, propriety, and legitimacy. To argue that "legitimacy" is questionable be-cause it represses and maintains something it claims to abhor certainly targets the hypocrisy in these odious adjudications, but importantly and despite this, it remains committed to the narrative's political order and its conservative commitments—from primitive to civilized, from same to dif-ferent, from the maternal order to the paternal symbolic, from Nature to Culture. Why does Butler need to assume that Nature is inherently self-same, or that what we call Culture could not possibly be an expression of Nature's own internal differentiations?

To posit the social or cultural as a second-order frame of reference, a regulating force that befalls the infant (who initially lacks it) and leaves it at a loss, understands identity as "something" that is either present *or* absent, true *or* fictional. To congeal the process of differentiation into a circum-scribable commodity or system, secured against an outside, is the same as reifying the phallus, the process of identify*ing*, into a thing—the penis. Can the ingenious provocation that Butler offers us in "the lesbian phallus" keep this question of origins moving, and in a way that might resist a return to identity's fixed and foundational truth? Does the open-ended sense of possibility and entanglement in Butler's argument really need to ascribe to an incest taboo that confers legitimacy through prohibition, and recuperates the *cogito* as always and only human—not natural? What if power's original and ongoing purpose, its *natural* intention, is always/al-ready multiple, contrary, disseminated, incestuous? Surely power can only fail to achieve its purpose, its goal, if it has "one" (repression).[15]

6. Culpability and the Double-Cross

Irigaray with Merleau-Ponty

By way of introduction I would like to say something about feminism's formative importance to my argument's overall commitments and sensibility, yet in a way that might illustrate why the accepted protocols that have come to define feminism's identity, authority, and authorship might be in need of reconsideration.

When I first began reading continental criticism and philosophy some twenty-five years ago, I consumed it as if I had been waiting all my life for its special form of nourishment. Perhaps it was the implication of revaluing "the negative"—the supposedly useless, primordial, superfluous, or denigrated—that felt so intellectually invigorating and politically and personally transformative. The promise, put simply, was that we could reconceive ourselves by contesting the negative's presumed deficiency. It seemed uncanny, the way that the political inequities that separate and define people should be mirrored in the binary structuration of language, a structure whose hidden system of accounting always equated "otherness" with corporeal incapacity—feminized, racialized, broken, and somehow wrong. What fascinated me most was the sense that some sort of "connective tissue" enabled the process of signification and its valuations to animate lived, corporeal perception and bodily being. Indeed, it was the conviction that there was a productive enfolding of language with life that gave the ontology of language, and discursive analysis more generally, a much broader political relevance.

At that time, I found Luce Irigaray's two major works, *This Sex Which Is*

Not One (1985a) and *Speculum of the Other Woman* (1985b) quite inspiring in their exploration of language's resonating impact on existential possibilities. Irigaray's argument concerned the phallocentrism of Western thought and the way its insidious binary logic represents woman as a failed man rather than as a subject in her own right. In sum, the conceptual infrastructure in language that understands the differences between, for example, Nature and Culture, body and mind, simple and complex, black/ignorance and white/enlightenment, and so on is sexually and racially inflected. It is as if there is a linear unfolding, a narrative order that posits one side of the divide as feminized *because* primitive, while the other side is necessarily more evolved and cut off from its primordial origins *because* male. These tautologous logics are ubiquitous and cross-contaminating. For this reason, Irigaray argues that the struggle for equity will be disappointed, as it unwittingly installs man as the reference point against which woman's capacities and achievements should be measured. Given this dilemma, the ingenious tactic that Irigaray brings to bear on this problem captured my interest. Irigaray's argument was unusual because it was able to take its shape from the very contours of phallocentrism's self-definition. The signature of her intervention is a form of mimicry, a loving "espousal of the philosophers," as Carolyn Burke describes it in "Irigaray through the Looking Glass," because in its close attention to the openings and folds of these phallocentric logics her perverse form of fidelity discloses the value of their repressed and disavowed interiorities.

Irigaray's painstaking care with these discourses is especially instructive because her ability to find transgressive leverage *from within them* achieved two very important things. First, her discovery of a difference "on the inside" of phallocentrism effectively shifts our understanding of its denigrating energies and oppositional agonistics: it contests the very possibility of an identical self-sameness and an absolute prohibition. Apparently, it is not just woman who is incoherent. And second, if man is no longer intact as the solid reference point against which woman's insufficiency can be measured, then "this sex which is not one" cannot be ascribed to just one sex and one name—"Woman." Irigaray's careful interrogation of subject formation and identity persuaded me that although all conceptual bifurcations articulate with, and reinforce, a normative sexual diacritics, the stability of their identifying coordinates and cross-referencing is profoundly compromised. Inevitably and yet surprisingly, it is from inside the very structural architecture that sustains these constraining logics that we come upon the surprise of Dr. Who's *Tardis*, a place whose interior dimensions promise different and unexpected accommodations and ways of being.

As I read the nuances of Irigaray's work during that heady time and discovered that a seemingly phallocentric text can prove a useful tool with myriad applications/readings, it appeared that Irigaray's methods were not unrelated to the strategies adopted by Jacques Derrida. Derrida did not define the *bricoleur*—the creative invention of the handyman who adapts his box of tools to his own specific purposes—against the engineer, as Claude Lévi-Strauss had done. For Derrida, the freedom, or "play" in a system, is not something external, something that arrives from elsewhere, for it arises in the very movement, or frisson, of a system's own internal operations. Given this, Derrida's insistence that there is no outside logocentrism is not meant to justify political quietism; after all, according to this logic feminism and other contestatory political programs are born within the interstices of logocentrism's commitments and practices. Derrida's provocation, rather, is the discovery that a different economy of valuation, indeed, different worlds, can be found within the very "scene" from which we might hope to escape. In sum, the resonance between Irigaray's and Derrida's approaches—a politics that worked with contamination and confusion rather than one that hankered for thinly disguised forms of purity and redemption—held great appeal.

However, today, Irigaray's foundational and motivating claim that sexual difference is irreducible seems misguided, or strangely static, given the evidence of utter ambiguity that surrounds all identity, an insight that actually enables the very strategies that Irigaray herself so cleverly deploys. What I hope to offer in my dilation on this "conversation" between Irigaray and Maurice Merleau-Ponty is an illustration of how feminism's identity, indeed, all identity, is necessarily fragile and contingent, and why feminism's promiscuous appearance in unexpected places and forms might be something we seek to encourage and engage rather than defend against.

Luce Irigaray's *An Ethics of Sexual Difference* (1993) is an ambitious project that explores this subject's feminine morphology. Irigaray explains the difficulty in reconceiving justice as well as the reasons why the overwhelming extent of the undertaking underlines its urgency. If our sense of "right" rests on a natural devaluation and erasure of the feminine and the female subject, as Irigaray suggests—for example, justice and reason are achieved by devaluing and transcending corporeal demands and connections such as affect and its domestic registers—and if it is through this erasure and denigration that we determine what is true, logical, and just, then how are we to acknowledge the priority and consequence of this grounding injustice? Given the reach of the problem, Irigaray opens her discussion of sexual difference by emphasizing the necessity of a thorough overhaul in how we think this issue: "We need to reinterpret everything concerning the relations between the subject and discourse, the subject and the world, the subject and the cosmic, the microcosmic and the macrocosmic. Everything, beginning with the way in which the subject has always been written in the masculine form, as *man*, even when it claimed to be universal or neutral" (1993, 6). For Irigaray then, the identity of the subject as well as the identity of every Western subject and discourse, is "always *masculine and paternal*" (1993, 6–7). Thus, Irigaray's conviction that the coordinates of our existence are organized around "the subject, the master of time, [as] the axis of the world's ordering" (1993, 7), makes her call for a global rearrangement of things an imperative one.

Given its pivotal importance for her argument as well as for a considerable amount of contemporary analysis, I want to focus on Irigaray's critique of the subject, especially her understanding of the relationship between the subject and language, and the subject and the maternal. Maurice Merleau-Ponty also offers a re-visioning of the feminine and the maternal as he refuses the orthodoxy of the mind/body split, wherein materiality, or corporeality, is something to be detached from, and transcended by, cognition. In the *Visible and the Invisible* (1968), he calls for a nondualistic ontology and embarks on "an ontology from within" (1968, 237), indeed, an "intra-ontology" as Françoise Dastur describes it (2000, 33). Irigaray certainly approves the direction of Merleau-Ponty's efforts in this, his last work, and devotes a chapter to its analysis in *An Ethics*. However, although both writers appear to be exploring the same subject and to desire a similar outcome, important, and perhaps irreconcilable, differences do emerge that illuminate their different commitments.

Irigaray differentiates the feminine against masculinity, yet *within* the identity of humanity proper, attempting to wrest the maternal from its patriarchal confinement. In contrast to Merleau-Ponty's blanket notion of "the flesh of the world," a notion whose apparent neutrality Irigaray will contest, she offers the "maternal-feminine." The special power of this term, as Tina Chanter explains, is that "the French word *féminin* does not carry with it the largely cultural connotations of the English 'feminine,' but rather designates at the same time the female sex. The maternal-feminine, like the notion of the flesh, can therefore be understood neither exclusively in terms of culture, nor entirely in terms of nature. It precisely brings into question the ease with which such categories take on their meaning" (2000, 227).

In contrast to this, Merleau-Ponty conjures the feminine and the maternal in terms of a much larger question of genesis, for his purpose is to reconceive the subject of humanity itself, the Human no less, through the body of Nature. Merleau-Ponty refers to the productive context of humanity's delivery as "the flesh of the world," and clearly, this process of conception cannot be confined to woman. Nevertheless, Irigaray regards Merleau-Ponty's global and implicated dispersal of the subject as an appropriation of feminine attributes, such that the double-cross that corrupts and divides the identity of the maternal from itself, thereby lending it to everything, becomes a sign of moral failure and culpability for Irigaray, a barrier that prevents an ethics of sexual difference from being articulated. Given the censoriousness of Irigaray's criticisms, I want to explain why I regard Merleau-Ponty's double-cross as an essential ingredient in the very possibility of an ethics of any sort. In the argument that follows I will explore some of the implications that attend Irigaray's circumscription of the feminine and the maternal and try to suggest how the "issue" of conception might be given quite differently.

For Irigaray, the question of the maternal orients us toward questions about history and origins. It recalls a time in which the gift of life as well as its nurturing maintenance was first received in that original dwelling place. And yet it involves much more than this scene of debt and nostalgia conventionally concedes. Irigaray warns that nostalgia is a major obstacle to any significant reconsideration of an ethics of sexual difference because it "blocks the threshold of the ethical world" (1993, 142). At first glance, this may seem like a curious judgment given Irigaray's own attempts to articulate a return that will acknowledge the importance of the past and our ongoing debt to it. And yet it makes sense that this temporal reflex, or going back, will not be straightforward if, as she suggests, "we must reconsider the whole problematic of *space* and *time*" (1993, 7). In view of this larger requirement, how might the temporality of nostalgic return and the place it has conventionally come to occupy for us actually hamper or block this possibility?

Irigaray compares the structure of nostalgia to an edifice. It is a building whose architecture witnesses man's rather fretful compulsion to discover and reconnect with his "living roots" (1993, 142). The frenzied tempo and obsessive pathos of its construction is, however, evidence of something else that remains hidden behind its outward facade, namely, man's anxieties about the carnality of his own history. Man's need to grasp and commodify the origin, his need to render it accessible and controllable while nevertheless maintaining it safely in the past, is a protective maneuver that denies the origin in the very act of an apparent recognition. As man circles around himself in a repeated attempt to return to the maternal and again recover that original space, "he surrounds himself with envelopes, containers, 'houses' which prevent him from finding either the other or himself" (1993, 142). Irigaray generalizes this observation, epitomizing man as "forever searching for, building, creating homes for himself everywhere: caves, huts, women, cities, language, concepts, theory, and so on" (1993, 141). Thus Culture itself is diagnosed as an inherently masculine set of endeavors and attributes, where "*to inhabit* is the fundamental trait of man's being" (1993, 141).

Nostalgia works to protect the masculine subject by burying his true foundations, re-membering his world by cutting it off from "the threshold, the flesh" (1993, 141). As a result, "man has built himself a world that is largely uninhabitable. A world in his image? An uninhabitable functional body? Like the technical world and all its sciences. Or like the scientific world and all its techniques" (1993, 143). Scientific inquiry becomes an instrumental form of knowledge in this account, a mode of cutting up and dismembering the world into usable and manageable parts. And Irigaray insists that such modes of inquiry are a direct reflection of a very particular way of being in the world, a way of being that has forgotten its indebtedness to history and to the connectivity of existence. It seems that man's very style of reflection and the way he engages and manages his place in the world recapitulate the alienated relationship he has to his own flesh. "Cut into parts like a mechanical body" (1993, 143), he removes himself from himself in order to maintain a semblance of control. With no "organic rhythm" (1993, 143) to unite him, both the body of man and the body of his world are severed from themselves. The inevitable result is that the nature of corporeal substance can only be recognized at a distance, in the triumphant guise of scientific mastery and machinic usefulness.

But there is a way out of this alienated space that is perhaps, at the same time, a more interesting way into it (the spatial metaphorics are increasingly ambiguous). Irigaray wonders if perhaps a different sense of space might be offered through "the usual dimension of the feminine" (1993, 141): "Staying out in the open, always attuned to the outside, to the world" (141), the sensate body of perception offers Irigaray a way back that is not an archaeology of return. Instead of the rather constipated and closed scene of controlled production that is Culture, perception is read as mobile, active, and generous by nature. "Senses always alert" (141), perception both opens and gives itself without qualification. "To perceive, to remain within the perception of the world without closing it off or closing off the self, amounts to forming or watching over the *threshold* of the world" (141). Irigaray aligns this corporeal capacity for generosity, receptivity, and caring with the subject position of woman and the feminine: "women, who, it seems, remain within perception without need of name or concept. Without closure" (141). The interrogative mood of Irigaray's writing is clearly sympathetic to this rather enigmatic description, for it allows the female subject to remain elusive in the face of an intense examination of the nature of her being. Irigaray is not concerned to provide a more accurate representation of woman, but rather to question the definitional constraints that normally find her lacking. It would appear that an ethics of sexual difference will only be possible if the syllogism that equates woman with negativity and passivity is thoroughly reconstrued and revalued.

Irigaray's discussion of Merleau-Ponty's quite remarkable essay "The Intertwining—The Chiasm," provides a more detailed sense of why this revaluation of the feminine is needed and how the process might unfold. Merleau-Ponty is an especially fitting philosopher to think with here because as mentioned above, many of his concerns share an apparent resonance with Irigaray's. *The Visible and the Invisible* (1968), for example, a posthumous collection of writings that includes "The Intertwining," represents Merleau-Ponty's most suggestive meditation on the phenomenology of perception, a sort of phenomenology of phenomenology. His radical reinvention of the terms of this approach signal a major assault on our most routine notions about subjectivity, as well as the frame within which an antihumanist critique of the subject is usually mounted. Merleau-Ponty confounds the division between ideality and materiality, Culture and Nature, and even the clear separation of the human from its "other," when he describes the world itself as "the flesh," thus imbuing it with the subtle intelligence usually reserved for human subjectivity. The flesh of the world can be regarded as sensible in every possible way because its perception of itself is an experience of the will to self-knowledge. By recasting the question of subjectivity as "the flesh," that is, as a worldly becoming, Merleau-Ponty is suggesting that there can be no final arrival any more than there can be a single atomic origin, or beginning. This would mean, for example, that "humanness" is not an entity *in* the world, as if in a container that is ontologically separate from the world: humanness could not justify its exceptionalism by claiming a special capacity for intellection in an inchoate universe. Rather, the world, *by implication*, would always have been in the process of discovering, exploring, redefining, and reinventing the nature of its humanity.

By beginning with the global capacity of "the flesh" to embrace itself, a reflex that Merleau-Ponty calls "reversibility," we can understand why the very process of perception for Merleau-Ponty must be a form of self-encounter. But how are we to understand this comprehensive and comprehending "Self"? The philosopher explains that within the expansive corporeal personification of "the Sensible," the difference between birth and thought, substance and form, body and mind, and origin and outcome takes on a transitive collapse. A sense of the maternal is certainly at the heart of the issue, as Merleau-Ponty acknowledges when he comments in "Working Notes," "Nature: it is the flesh, the mother" (1968, 267). However, Merleau-Ponty's attempt to read the maternal as the world's "intertwining," or (re)conceiving (of) itself, represents a complete dislocation of the temporal and spatial coordinates through which maternity is *properly* identified.

As we saw above, Irigaray predicates the possibility of an ethics of sexual difference on the need for this reexamination, suggesting, "We must reconsider the whole problematic of *space* and *time*" (1993, 7). Yet despite the apparent commonality in their arguments, Irigaray finds Merleau-Ponty's notional disruption along these very lines to be seriously misguided. She judges the philosopher's rampant dispersal of maternity into the generalized and generative capacity of "the flesh" a displacement and erasure of the specificity of the feminine, and one that inevitably discounts maternity in the conventional sense. But does Merleau-Ponty's insistence on the ecological[1] dimensions of the birth scene preclude an appreciation of specificity, of perceptual situatedness? Does it reduce everything to homogeneity and "a logic of the same"? Indeed, given the presumption of specificity that drives Irigaray's argument, we will need to ask if her own blanket notion—"logic of the same"—actually discounts the possibility of specificity in places where she diagnoses a relentless, normative homogeneity. We will return to this question.

As we have seen, Irigaray aligns perception with the feminine and confirms this morphological connection by privileging metaphors of "openness." As a consequence, openness (to the difference of others) is read as a gesture of generosity, a way of being that promises more hopeful and generative futures for all parties. The implicit moralism in any conceptual duality is uncritically deployed here, and, as a consequence, the very notion of closure becomes a synonym for what is threatening and destructive, or what holds itself back from the good and the creative. And yet, Merleau-Ponty will find a way to ameliorate even this agonistic face-off about how we should move forward. Importantly for this discussion, he also figures perception through the feminine, as is evident in his quite specific use of the term "invagination" to describe how the flesh of the world folds back upon itself in an interrogative reflex. For Merleau-Ponty then, the world perceives itself by opening itself to the experience of its own difference— the energies, torsions, contrasts, and tensions of its noncoincidence. In its very directness, the intention of this global embrace (invagination) is to seize the essential fullness of Being *in all its expressions*. And in its desire for carnal knowledge it follows that "the flesh" is unashamedly lacking in reserve: the wantonness of its desire is so diverse, so perverse, so focused, and yet also distracted, that even when it seems to withdraw into itself, holding itself close against its own inquiry, it nevertheless remains in touch with itself.

It is important to appreciate that the generosity of Merleau-Ponty's reworking of phenomenology is so thoroughly comprehensive in its unqualified openness to the world that even closure is intrinsic to its makeup. In other words, the relation of the flesh to itself is such that it incorporates all of the dualities and negations, the moral judgments and admonitions, that would conventionally be assumed either to fall outside it, or to operate as independent entities or forces against it. Put simply, the flesh cannot be defined against closure, for closing, sealing, and separating are intrinsic to its desire for itself: the differentiation or individuation of itself from itself. In this regard, closure is not so much a denial, or absolute bar of prohibition, as it is an internal movement, or differential *of* "the flesh."

Merleau-Ponty's re-vision of the Sensible tries to acknowledge something of this internal divergence of the flesh, a dissonance, or *écart* as he calls it, where perception becomes self-interrogation. His notion of the maternal, and by implication, his understanding of the feminine, should be read in terms of this generalized scene of corporeal inquiry. The debt to the maternal opens the question of becoming and is clearly of crucial importance to Merleau-Ponty's project. However, for Merleau-Ponty, the generative nature of the Sensible, its ability to reproduce itself, is such that it undoes maternity's spatial and temporal location as straightforwardly in the past, in a single, identifiable place and moment of time, and given by only one body, one gender, and through one sexual act. Indeed, the gift of birth for Merleau-Ponty, the foundation of what is given, is not likened to an economic transaction, a unidirectional transfer of a living debt that can never be repaid because it happened in the past. Perception is instead likened to an ontological organ of *con*ception. It is a desiring organ that seizes upon its own alienness, and in the wonder of the encounter, is reconceived. The doubled sense of conception that couples knowledge with birth, epistemology emerging as the entanglement of ontology, is therefore inextricably alive in this perverse intercourse whose subject is "a question consonant with the porous being which it questions and from which it obtains not an *answer*, but a confirmation of its astonishment" (1968, 102). For Merleau-Ponty, then, existence is gestation, where this "new type of being" is "a being by porosity, pregnancy, or generality, and he before whom the horizon opens is caught up, included within it. His body and the distances participate in one same corporeity or visibility in general, which reigns between them and it, and even beyond the horizon, beneath his skin, unto the depths of being" (1968, 149).

The volubility of "the flesh" in its turning back upon itself, in its chiasmic reversibility, is not an act of nostalgic mourning for one origin, now irretrievably lost. Rather, it is the dehiscence, or bursting open, of the origin itself in its infinite iterations. This explains why Merleau-Ponty's elaboration of perception is not dependent upon a notion of the subject or self that, however seemingly primordial and temporally prior, must preexist in some foundational way the capacity to engage the world fully. Although this assumption is evident in his earlier work, in, for example, *The Phenomenology of Perception* (1962), Merleau-Ponty's radical reflection on the notions of consciousness and subjectivity leads to its remarkable rearticulation. An extended passage from *Signs* (1995) that tentatively muses about different directions illustrates the general intention his work began to realize, and is suggestive for how we might read "The Intertwining":

> Take *others* at the moment they appear in the world's flesh. They would not exist for me, it is said, unless I recognized them, deciphering in them some sign of the presence to self whose sole model I hold within me. But though my thought is indeed only the other side of my times, of my passive and perceptible being, whenever I try to understand myself the whole fabric of the perceptible world comes too, and with it come the others who are caught in it. Before others are or can be subjected to my conditions of possibility and reconstructed in my image, they must already exist as outlines, deviations, and variants of a single Vision in which I too participate. For they are not fictions with which I might people my desert—offspring of my spirit and forever unactualized possibilities—but my twins or the flesh of my flesh. Certainly I do not live their life; they are definitively absent from me and I from them. But that distance becomes a strange proximity as soon as one comes back home to the perceptible world, since the perceptible is precisely that which can haunt more than one body without budging from its place. No one will see that table which now meets my eye; only I can do that. And yet I know that at the same moment it presses upon every glance in exactly the same way. For I see these other glances too. Within the same field with things they sketch out a dis-position of the table, linking its parts together for a new compresence. (1995, 15–16)

There is something profoundly moving in the intimacy of this shared horizon of emergence; this semiosis of ontological differentiation through which the flesh of the world experiences and understands itself. The implosion of spacetime that the vitalism of this chiasmic contagion represents is extraordinary because whatever we might posit as preexistent in Nature is, still, in the process of becoming itself. For Merleau-Ponty, this insight is not the ideality of philosophical abstraction as it is conventionally understood. Indeed, the importance of what he is trying to articulate here is also acknowledged by Irigaray herself when she opens her discussion of "The Intertwining—The Chiasm" with the philosopher's own words: "If it is true that as soon as philosophy declares itself to be reflection or coincidence it prejudges what it will find, then once again it must recommence everything, reject the instruments reflection and intuition had provided themselves, and install itself in a locus where they have not yet been distinguished, in experiences that have not yet been 'worked over,' that offer us all at once, pell-mell, both 'subject' and 'object,' both existence and essence, and hence give philosophy resources to redefine them" (1993, 151).

Despite the acknowledgment that immediately follows this quotation, namely, that "up to this point, my reading and my interpretation of the history of philosophy agree with Merleau-Ponty" (151), Irigaray is also signaling that she will soon part company with him. One example of the tensions between their arguments can be seen in Irigaray's need to define this "locus" of presumed harmony where oppositional determinations and their political baggage "have not yet been distinguished." Her gloss on these words turns into the imperative: "We must go back to a moment of prediscursive experience" (151). However, Merleau-Ponty's sense of a return that will nevertheless acknowledge these contraries "all at once, pell-mell" is not at all a straightforward appeal to a sense of temporality that separates out into atomic moments of past, present, and future, as the priority of a prediscursive must assume. His argument is not reliant on an unfolding sense of linear time that necessarily installs a prelapsarian "before," with the inevitable nostalgia and moral lamentation that such an appeal evokes, and that, as we have seen, Irigaray herself eschews when she attributes its displaced manifestations to male desire. And this makes sense if we remember that Merleau-Ponty's notion of the feminine, and maternity too, is an interrogative one, where identity is both opened and dispersed through the *question* of existence and becoming. Quite clearly, Merleau-Ponty is not at all interested in resolving the identity of what is proper to a subjective locus of sexual difference, "as if one already knew what to exist is and as if the whole question were to apply this concept appropriately" (1968, 6).

The philosophers' quite different intentions are again made apparent in Irigaray's "Love of the Other," the essay that immediately precedes her discussion of "The Intertwining" in *An Ethics of Sexual Difference*. There she evokes what is positive and somehow necessary for all of us in recovering this originary space of "the before." It is "[a] zone of calm and respite from the race toward productivity. . . . Something that resists dispersion, diaspora, the explosion of the flesh or of the incarnation" (1993, 143–44). More telling still, Irigaray's sense of what is vital, well, and good is elided with the ability, first of all, to cohere, and *then* to connect, an ability that she identifies with tactility. If tactility joins and remembers it seems that vision dissects and forgets. For Irigaray then, splitting as such is equated with a sense of violence against an originary integrity, a position that can be explained by her commitment, however critical, to a psychoanalytic understanding of subject formation. Put simply, the child's birth, or entrance into Culture, is achieved through the loss and then the denigration of that (m)othered part of itself. The moral tenor in Irigaray's argument rests on an urgent attempt to stall what she regards as the rapidly approaching cataclysm that will be realized by man's love of technological and scientific dissection. Warning against this dissolution into the machinic, Irigaray comments, "Nietzsche thought of the subject as an atom. This atom will be split if it fails to find some life-enhancing rhythm" (1993, 144).

Yet Merleau-Ponty finds this "life enhancing rhythm" in the very ability of "the flesh" to perceive and center itself *in its dispersion.* In other words, there never was an atom, an individual, to be split, as all identity is given chiasmically. Dispersion can be read as maternity here because the issuing forth of any identity is an involvement that is present across space and time: it must incorporate the (w)hole of "the flesh." This need not mean, however, that we are unable to acknowledge a particular location, or "condensation" of conception and emergence. What is so remarkable in Merleau-Ponty's reverie that "no one will see that table which now meets my eye; only I can do that," is that the very "here-and-nowness" of his singular experience can only be actualized, or validated, because "*at the same moment* it presses upon every glance in exactly the same way" (emphasis added).

For Merleau-Ponty, a field that is unified by the enduring intention to differentiate itself does not prohibit particularity. As noted, spacetime enfolding is not made up of atomic entities—something unique and particular here and then something quite separate and different again over there—but of coordinates whose "compresence" evokes the whole of the world as "the flesh" takes measure of itself . . . differently. The body's senses are suggestively described as "*measurants (mesurants)* for Being, dimensions to which we can refer it, but not a relation of adequation or of immanence" (1968, 103). As this is a wild and counterintuitive logic that Merleau-Ponty calls upon to explain perception and phenomena, it is worth noting its quantum implications here.

Merleau-Ponty splits the atom of identity in all its forms—whether the observing subject, the observed object, or even the identity of an "in-between" that appears to mark their separation into agent, instrument, representation, or model. His dispersal of the subject is evocative, likening the motions of its becoming an "entity" (an individual, a particle of sorts) to the spreading movement and expansive pull and undertow of a wave:

> If we can show that the flesh is an ultimate notion, that it is not the union or compound of two substances, but thinkable by itself, if there is a relation of the visible with itself that traverses me and constitutes me as a seer, this circle which I do not form, which forms me, this coiling over of the visible upon the visible, can traverse, animate other bodies as well as my own. And if I was able to understand how this wave arises within me, how the visible which is yonder is simultaneously my landscape, I can understand a fortiori that elsewhere it also closes over upon itself and that there are other landscapes besides my own. (1968, 140–41)

We could add here, other landscapes whose special contours are not entirely unknown to me (the notion of knowledge is being opened here, rather than extended) as my very existence is a reversible synergy. Although the magical poesis of Merleau-Ponty's descriptions are perhaps more suggestive than descriptive, what we can say unequivocally is that the philosopher's attempt to conjure the complex nature of the subject's emergence is not positioned *against the feminine*, as Irigaray insists. For Merleau-Ponty it would make no sense to defend the integrity of the feminine, or indeed, any other "corporeity," and to claim that its identity should or could be circumscribed, maintained, and defended against its improper use.

If the radical interiority of the Sensible is utterly referential then we can understand why Merleau-Ponty's notion of identity, or self-possession, has a quite peculiar dimensional density. He posits the workings of perceptual registration as an implicated weave, or language, that "holds with all its fibers onto the fabric of the visible, and thereby onto a fabric of invisible being" (132). Whether in the instance of a perceptual moment or in the existence of a perceiving being, identity for Merleau-Ponty is "a certain node in the woof of the simultaneous and the successive. It is a concretion of visibility, it is not an atom" (132). Merleau-Ponty therefore corporealizes semiosis such that "the flesh" is articulate in its perceptions and in contact with itself through autodispersion. However, it is precisely here, in this collapse and dispersal of both the subject and language in/as "the flesh," that Irigaray discovers a masculinist reductionism. I want to focus on the reasoning behind this charge in order to suggest why Irigaray's critique might be misguided, and why the importance of her own efforts might be furthered rather than hindered by Merleau-Ponty's quite exquisite feel for the intricacy and wonder in this seemingly simple word, "language." Ironically perhaps, I will argue that Irigaray's irritations with Merleau-Ponty take their strength from that same nostalgic desire for self-presence that elsewhere she describes as "block[ing] the threshold of the ethical world" (1993, 142).

The following comment by Merleau-Ponty provides us with some appreciation of how he conceives an ontological discourse, a becoming sensible: "If we were to make completely explicit the archetectonics of the human body, its ontological framework, and how it sees itself and hears itself, we would see that the structure of its mute world is such that all the possibilities of language are already given in it" (1968, 155). Accordingly, the nature of the phenomenological world, its "*langue*," is neither prior to the technology of the word, nor subsumed to its supposed abstractions. Rather, it is the implicate order of an intertwining, something whose enfoldings are reminiscent of what is implied by "entanglement" in contemporary physics—a living ground.

The reason why I continue to mention the shared implications between these seemingly unrelated scholarly endeavors and their very different disciplinary objects and methodologies is because what purportedly separates the ideational from the physical entirely collapses, and for similar reasons, in the respective notions of intertwining and entanglement. Importantly, the sense of an "in-between" preexisting entities, the sense of space or time that localizes and divides reality into measurable definitions of classical containment, simply doesn't obtain in Merleau-Ponty's revision, nor in current evidence of quantum complexity.[2] Does this calling up of scientific evidence and the debates that it provokes have any relevance for Irigaray's argument regarding the specific location of the feminine—the qualities, capacities, and sensibilities that seem hidden, forgotten, or somehow inaccessible?

Funnily enough, in the lamentations of Albert Einstein over the apparent fact of nonlocality we hear echoes of Irigaray's complaint against Merleau-Ponty. The reason for Einstein's unease was the increasingly persuasive evidence that reality could not be divided into separate entities with specific properties, for it was strangely "in touch," or entangled. As mentioned in chapter 3, "spooky action at a distance" was Einstein's term for the peculiar behavioral correlations that obtained between what he regarded as individual entities that seemed to be "twinned," inasmuch as they were able to communicate across the vastness of space and time instantaneously—or faster than the speed of light. Faced with the dilemma of how to comprehend this paradox, Einstein comments, "I just want to explain what I mean when I say that we should try to hold on to physical reality. . . . That which we conceive as existing ('actual') should somehow be localized in time and space. That is, the real in one part of space, A, should (in theory) somehow 'exist' independently of that which is thought of as real in another part of space, B." And regarding the interference or observable changes that representation or measurement appears to effect, Einstein was adamant: "What is actually present in B should thus not depend upon the type of measurement carried out in the part of space, A; it should also be independent of whether or not, after all, a measurement is made in A" (quoted in Barad 2007, 319).

Despite the philosophical sophistication of Irigaray's argument, it is interesting to discover its shared commitment to Einstein's understanding of classical locality and identity, and to his belief that entities preexist their measurement or representation. Admittedly, Einstein did not have recourse to later experiments that would "confir[m] Bohr's central point that the objects and the agencies of observation are inseparable parts of a single phenomenon" (Barad 2007, 315). The interesting point here is that Barad's description of Bohr's understanding is in rhythm with my reading of Merleau-Ponty.

As the paradox that confounded Einstein and provoked his consternation has logical symmetry with certain of Irigaray's foundational commitments to space, time, and causality, and as the following passage eloquently and clearly captures what is at stake in this difficult puzzle, I will quote it at length. The context is Karen Barad's exposition of why our sense of a reality made up of individual objects—and this, of course, includes subjects—fails to appreciate that we are dealing with "phenomena" whose very being is always and only an articulation of entanglement. In the two-slit experiment to determine whether light behaves as wave or particle, "the atom is not a separate object but rather an inseparable part of the phenomenon (that includes the micromaser cavities, the photodetector-shutter system, the double slit defraction grating, and the screen among other elements)"

(2007, 315). Commenting on the delayed-choice aspect of this experiment, where the experimenter makes his/her decision about the measuring apparatus *after* the "object" has passed the point of measurement, in other words, once, we might assume, the specificity of whatever it is (particle or wave) has already arrived and is therefore in evidence, Barad notes:

> If one focuses on abstract individual entities the result is an utter mystery, we cannot account for the seemingly impossible behavior of the atoms. It's not that the experimenter changes a past that had already been present or that atoms fall in line with a new future simply by erasing information. The point is that the past was never simply there to begin with and the future is not simply what will unfold; the "past" and the "future" are iteratively reworked and enfolded through the iterative practices of spacetimemattering—including the which slit detection and the subsequent erasure of which slit information—all are *one phenomenon*. There is no spooky-action-at-a-distance co-ordination between individual particles separated in space or individual events separated in time. Space and time are phenomenal, that is, they are intra-actively produced in the making of phenomena; neither space nor time exist as determinate givens outside of phenomena. (315)

Returning to Merleau-Ponty, we see this same understanding of phenomenal complexity—phenomenal reality—when he insists that the material ground of the senses (Nature) does not constitute a realm that can be violated by its imperfect translation into the separate linguistic register of the ideal (Culture). His reworking of language therefore shares the Derridean conviction that what grounds, and indeed *is* language, is the brain-twisting suggestion of difference itself; not the difference between one thing and another, but a process that gives rise to the perception of an event as a divided phenomenon. Importantly then, what we understand by "language" significantly departs from convention when we acknowledge that the ground of reference and what we routinely perceive and comprehend as substance is already *intrinsic* to its systematicities: "The meaning is not on the phrase like the butter on the bread, like a second layer of 'psychic reality' spread over the sound: it is the totality of what is said, the integral of all the differentiations of the verbal chain; it is given with the words for those who have ears to hear. And conversely the whole landscape is overrun with words" (1968, 155). Merleau-Ponty concludes his thesis by recalling Paul Valéry's insight that language is a sort of contagion: "Language is everything, since it is the voice of no one, since it is the very voice of the things, the waves, and the forests" (155).

Essential to Merleau-Ponty's argument is the sense that meaning involves disjunction, as it is "something" that emerges as the global subject learns "*to hear what it says (l'entendre)*" (155). The phrase evokes a sort of narcissistic focus wherein the world attends to itself, as if fascinated by its own variation —an ongoing internal dialogue. But why should Merleau-Ponty describe the whole of this corporeal tissue of the Sensible, with all its perceptual styles and modalities, as "the Visible"? Irigaray is understandably critical of this apparent privileging of the eye, with its phallogocentric thematizations—the privileged validation of observation in terms of a disinterested distance; the valorization of instrumental reason whose very operations require the transcendance of one's subjective, corporeal situation. However, this "touch-vision system," as Merleau-Ponty calls it, is intricacy itself. Perception becomes a relational enfolding where, for example, "a certain blue of the sea is so blue that only blood would be more red" (1968, 132). Thus, Merleau-Ponty imbues Vision with a sort of wild associational and synaesthetic conversion, a supersaturation within and across all perceptual modalities, such that we hear visually, taste aurally, and so on.

This reconfigured expansiveness that is always/already operative in any individuation means that "Visibility" can be read in much the same way as Jacques Derrida's "textuality," or "general writing." It is important to recall that Derrida does not delineate, or privilege, writing over speech when he describes speech as writing. However, his intervention does destabilize what is taken as an anchor for the difference between these two modes of expression. Derrida's reversal effects an interrogation of why speech and writing are interpreted through the bipolar template of origin to supplement, simple to complex, corporeal truth and purity to the contagious retrovirus of intellectual corruption. We could add here (as it is this founding division that informs the nostalgic imperative in Irigaray's own argument), Nature to Culture, with the feminine as primordial and generative and the masculine as secondary and instrumental. Interestingly, and despite Merleau-Ponty's complex elaboration of what he means by "Visibility," Irigaray seems intent on diagnosing the curious ambiguities in his position as simply erroneous.

Merleau-Ponty's corporeal semiosis, this diverging rearticulation of "the flesh" from itself, completely fractures the self-presence of separate sensory modalities within one body, as well as the aggregation, or assembly, of separate, individual bodies within the body of the world. This amplification, which is also a form of condensation, is like a grammatology writ large. The ontological implications are apparent in a quite remarkable phrase from "The Experience of Others" (1982–83), where Merleau-Ponty says that "there is already a kind of presence of other people within me" (56). And again, from the same text, he remarks that "everything transpires as if the other person's intuitions and motor realizations existed in a sort of relation of internal encroachment, as if my body and the body of the other person together formed a system" (52). This grammatological intertwining of the flesh involves a fold that must continue to touch itself even as it opens itself up. And here we sense why Merleau-Ponty might generalize the fold of invagination right across the flesh of the world in order to evoke the contemporary nature of this generative coordination.

Irigaray erases what is *utterly* extraordinary in this reading of carnal speech, this generalized porosity of the "two lips," when she interprets it as a symptom of masculinist theft, correcting Merleau-Ponty's confusion between flesh and language by way of an excavation that promises to restore hierarchical order to the relationship. According to Irigaray, contact with the ur-ground of existence is no longer possible as it is lost beneath an archaeology of time. And yet, Irigaray advises against burying maternity in its original wrappings underneath the unfolding of history, as if it has no strings to the present. Indeed, for Irigaray, it is precisely this style of thinking that explains the denigration of maternity as an expendable moment whose value is quickly exhausted; as if the gift of life is dead and gone. Given these apparent contradictions, Irigaray determines to mount her intervention on two fronts. First, she argues that the past is a present that we continue to receive; and second, she insists that attempts to recuperate the originary moment of debt to maternity through its reification in the present actually bury and repress its specificity even more deeply. Her strategy, then, is to explore the differences between these positions in order to elaborate the need for a sexual ethics.

Nevertheless, although this doubled strategy strives to enliven our appreciation of time's implications, it is unable to disrupt our understanding of duration as a linear development of separate moments *in* time and *in* space—an archeology. Ironically perhaps, Irigaray's criticisms of Merleau-

Ponty's synaesthetic melding of the senses presume this same logic when they uncover tactility at the origin, in a space and time that identifies its precedence in the evolution of different sense modalities that have yet to come. Thus, her conclusion that "Merleau-Ponty accords an exorbitant privilege to vision" (1993, 174) is an inevitable one, given her premise that she is witnessing a "reduction of the tactile into the visible" (175). Already present at the origin, tactility becomes a perceptual ground and nurturing support, its difference feminized and isolated from what it bears: "The tangible is the matter and memory for all of the sensible. Which remembers without remembering thematically? It constitutes the very flesh of all things that will be sculpted, sketched, painted, felt, and so on, *out of it*" (164; emphasis added). In sum, Irigaray's understanding of maternity is that it gives but is not itself given because it is *the* given: it is not parented or constituted by anything other than itself. A pure, isolated, virgin birth.

Merleau-Ponty's Vision of maternity is wildly different from this because it does more than acknowledge an ongoing debt that *was* given, even as its effects are still being lived and felt. More than this, it seriously confounds the conventions of space and time that excavate an elementary transfer in an original place of inevitable demarcation. It grants that maternity is a gift that involves and revalues the future as well as the past, the generative capacities of men as well as women, and even the notions of vitality and efficacy that conventionally separate the animate from the inanimate. Whereas Merleau-Ponty's Vision *is* tactility, Irigaray's clarification marks a return to identity that assumes a primordial segregation. As Irigaray explains:

> In our language, we are always basically idealists. Cut off from mother nature, where, whence, we are born, from our archaic state, our archives of flesh. Twisted "upon ourselves," but starting from a primary part of the self that is abandoned "with the other"—another feminine for both sexes. A part of the self does not come back to us in its primary-perception-reception. A part of our vitality that is buried, forgotten with the other, sometimes in the other, and which we receive with an other "voice," that of an ideal order (?) which covers us over. And which lacks voice, moreover. The text of the law, of codes, no longer has a voice. Even if it is in some way built upon the "model" of the voice. (1993, 169)

In this notion of the law as the distortion and even erasure of the voice, we witness an appeal to the self-presence of the origin in its pure immediacy; speech before writing. For Irigaray then, the voice (Nature, the body) is ruptured and violated from the outside, that is, by Culture and the language of the symbolic in its thematizations. Although flesh is engender-*ing* (maternal), it does not appear to be engender*ed* (parented) in Irigaray's argument. It is as if flesh precedes the rupture of copula-tion (becomings), as if, in simple terms, it just is. Irigaray does acknowledge that there is an internal movement, or differential at work within originary substance, yet its nature appears to be qualitatively different in that it remains wholesome even when it touches (others) itself.

Irigaray's presumption that the origin is sealed within itself such that it can only be broken open from the outside is a scene of sexual encounter that *must* define man as violating perpetrator. Perhaps men can violate each other, and they can certainly violate women, but according to this perspective it seems that women are simply incapable of such involved intercourse: a constitutional incapacity. It is as if the question of an ethics of sexual difference only arises in the heterosexual encounter, at the abyss that falls in-between two already separate identities, and as if the very determination of an identity and the presumption of its integrity is not already a scene of ethical consideration. According to Irigaray, an ethics of sexual difference questions how we encounter someone radically alien, someone whose existence is not just an inverted apparition of our own. But who are they, for themselves, in their own right? And why must we ground an ethics on the determination of a sexual priority, assuming we know what that is? If ontological difference involves thinking through the copula in its most general sense, then the nature of sexual difference must remain a question to be explored rather than a matter to be adjudicated.

In order to open the possibility of a "just" encounter, Irigaray argues that provision will need to be made for the maternal-feminine, because to date its specificity has been secreted away, entombed, and silenced. This will be necessary because if the difference of the feminine is not guarded against masculine appropriation (penetration), then the threshold of a true ethical encounter cannot be broached with safety. If it is not secured, then the inevitable outcome, as Irigaray sees it, is that the feminine will again appear in the guise of the same. However, if we return to Merleau-Ponty at this point, asking how he might proceed in the face of this possible impasse, we discover that Irigaray's metaphorics of purity and danger have been signifi-cantly reconceptualized. It is no longer a question of how the touch of alterity will be handled and kept on the "outside" as if penetration is improper, because for Merleau-Ponty, the ability of "the flesh" to touch itself on the outside is at the same time a penetration/investigation of itself from/on the inside. In other words, the very notion of violation is completely refigured in this inside/outside, space/time conversion/inversion if we do not begin with the assumption that identity is given whole from the start.

I want to explicate this point further by returning to the question of language. As witnessed above, these thinkers understand the identity and ontology of language very differently, and that difference permeates their entire *conceptual* project. Consistent with a Lacanian model of subject formation, Irigaray, for example, assumes that language (Culture) is *in* the world, as if it replaces the maternal origin of Nature from which it is now severed. It is a "kind of duplication or stand-in for the constitution of the flesh? A reversal of the maternal gift of flesh, in the autarchy of the subject of and in language" (1993, 179). Irigaray's description of "the dereliction of the lack in language" (1993, 180) would be apposite if it is indeed true that language is an "organism" or "system" that substitutes for something now lost to us, namely, our carnal beginnings. Despite this conventional reading and as Irigaray acknowledges, Merleau-Ponty's contribution is to refuse the division between the body (Nature) and language (Culture), and instead to comprehend carnality as thoroughly garrulous; as an originary vociferousness wherein "all the possibilities of language are already given" (Irigaray 1993, 180).

And here is the rub. Irigaray expresses a disapproving frustration with the fact that "there is no silence for Merleau-Ponty" (1993, 180), because she regards this internal dialogue of the flesh as a denial and repression of difference, as if the reversibility of language must remain a solipsism of sameness because it is no longer in touch with its carnal foundations. Interestingly, there is a momentary hesitation in Irigaray's negative judgment at this point, when she acknowledges something puzzling in Merleau-Ponty's insistence that an origin could be pregnant with language (180). Nevertheless, because Irigaray is bound to defend the circumscription of feminine identity and its corollaries, she is forced to conclude that Merleau-Ponty's framework of constitutive and gestatory reversibility is a topsy-turvy erasure of the feminine where "nothing new can be said" (180).

When we read Merleau-Ponty, however, it becomes clear that language cannot bear a severed relationship to the world if it is an expression *of* the world in its self-violation/self-evolution. Indeed, it is important to remember that the tactile is itself a language of differentiation and discrimination, as we see in the example of Braille, but more prosaically, in our ability to detect in pressures and textures a historicity whose referential diacritics constitute touch as sensate writing/reading. Touch is necessarily as differentiated/disrupted as any sensory modality, not just within itself, but because its "own" sense is also enlivened by an entire field of corporeal sensation.

Consistent with this notion that language is not a second-order representation or model of an absent world, but rather, an ontological energy through which the world makes itself known (to itself), witness Merleau-Ponty's musings about representations—indeed, drawings, maps, and their different scales and perspectives. Convention dictates that these drawings are substitutes for something that is itself not a drawing: we assume that the image is *derived* "from without," from a transcendent position that allows the representational proximations of observation that distance and difference provide. However, in the "Working Notes" section of *The Visible and the Invisible* Merleau-Ponty suggests that "it is a question of understanding that the 'views' at different scales are not projections upon corporeities—screens of an inaccessible In itself, that *they and their lateral implication in one another are the reality, exactly* [emphasis added]: that the reality is their common inner framework (*membrure*), their nucleus, and not something *behind them.* . . . Each field is dimensionality, and Being is dimensionality itself. It is therefore accessible indeed by my perception" (1968, 226–27). Merleau-Ponty's point here, and it repeats the same counterintuitive complexity that Barad captures in her descriptions of quantum entanglement, is that he can access the phenomenon—here, reality—because his looking, his desire to know, is implicated in the very ontology of what it is that he is looking at. The marvel in this refusal to locate the causal origin, or intention, that motors and explains this perceptual "event" is that the intention to look, the agency of observation, is as inherent in the "object" as it is in the "subject."

In a nutshell, language, representation, modeling—this is what the world does in its ongoing manufacture. Quite clearly, this sense of "violation"—of projections/introjections into self—is not a term that needs to imply something perilously dangerous, something to be condemned, any more than "corruption" must be interpreted as a moral flaw in this scene of genesis. In Merleau-Ponty's argument, where identity is utterly violated, we learn that corruption engenders. Masculinism could be said to mother feminism in the same gesture that discovers feminism, unwittingly perhaps, affirming masculinism. Similarly, appropriation is not simply theft but also birth. Importantly, and although Merleau-Ponty undoes the atomism of identity, this is no haphazard dissolution. Rather, Merleau-Ponty offers us a sense of how identity emerges through structured moments and rhythms of intercourse, where every act is *generally born*, and yet never in the same way. "Sameness," then, is no longer a burden, blocking the possibility of how we might think a sexual ethics in its radical difference, for radical alterity already inheres within the apparent unity and coherence of individual identity; consequently, sameness, as Irigaray understands it, is impossible. Irigaray reads the cut that Culture (masculinity) inflicts upon itself in an attempt to sever its relations with Nature (the feminine/the mother) in moral terms, as a wounding that is essentially and properly masculine because it comes from outside. However, if this fault line is chiasmatic and therefore fractured and dispersed, if it reappears ubiquitously and across the scale like a Mandelbrot filigree of repetitive transformation that is integral to all identity, then the entire universe is essentially at fault.

My reading of Merleau-Ponty's posthumous essay and its implications for the question of ethics starts and ends here, where no *one* is to blame. This is the difficulty of the question of ethics, namely, that it is and must remain a question that will continue to haunt our judgments. I am reminded here of Derrida's attempt to question the "purity and indivisibility" of the line that purportedly demarcates the human from the nonhuman. He anticipates the objections that will greet his argument because it upsets the ethical applecart and leaves us uncertain about how to proceed on many registers. His response to this concern is that, "casting doubt on responsibility, on decision, on one's own being-ethical, seems to me to be— and is perhaps what should forever remain—the unrescindable essence of ethics" (2003, 128). An ethics does not preclude blame nor deny violence in the ordinary sense; however, the realization that culpability cannot be attributed to any *one*, that it has no simple origin or cause, brings a more forgiving and generous sense of understanding to our adjudications, albeit one that will continue to concern us even after our political decisions have been made.

We will remember that Irigaray's call to action in the beginning of this chapter reads, "We need to reinterpret everything concerning the relations between the subject and discourse, the subject and the world, the subject and the cosmic, the microcosmic and the macrocosmic" (1993, 6). If we take this call seriously then it is not only the ground of the male subject that becomes unstable as his friable identity is acknowledged. Much more than this, the collective subject of Mankind also suffers a shock wave because our shared humanity and its unique capacities cannot be defined or enclosed against a nonhuman world of comparative insufficiency. Importantly, the resulting instability of these identities cannot be resolved with the corrective that replaces the sexism of Mankind with the more inclusive descriptor, Humankind.

One of the most destabilizing and, literally, wonderful passages in "The Intertwining" helps us here. As I read it, it does not repeat the conventional negative moves of either a humanist or an antihumanist critique, yet at the same time, given its inclusive sense of generosity, it need not dismiss them as simply mistaken. "When we speak of the flesh of the visible, we do not mean to do anthropology, to describe a world covered over with all our own projections, leaving aside what it can be under the human mask. Rather, we mean that carnal being, as a being of depths, of several leaves or several faces, a being in latency, and a presentation of a certain absence, is a prototype of Being, of which our body, the sensible sentient, is a very remarkable variant, but whose constitutive paradox already lies in every visible" (1968, 136). The challenge and charge in these words cannot be enlisted, at least in any straightforward way, to resolve the injustices of sexual discrimination, or racism, or even the long and ongoing histories of global exploitation. Indeed, the apportioning of culpability, however pragmatically necessary, if simply left at that will actually elide the complications in Merleau-Ponty's Vision. It will fail to acknowledge that behaviors, even when individual, are enabled by/through community. There are no true isolates. Thus, if the reversibility of the flesh is read as responsibility, then as suggested earlier, no *one* is to blame. All individuals and acts issue from "the flesh" of sexual difference—the constant process of realignment and renewal. "The Intertwining" explores the intricate nature, the ethical implications, of this involvement.

In sum, the negative associations that attend "the feminine," "the corporeal," and "woman" make much less sense if they cannot be contained as the primordial "other" of what comes next (Man, instrumental reason, Culture). And if we cannot identify woman as the impaired inversion of man then woman is not *the* origin/mother, a vessel to be broken into and out of, a figure whose fragility, violation, and comparative worthlessness are inevitable. Similarly, the identity of "man" will not locate *the* culprit who is driven to capitalize, denigrate, and destroy, for the political theater is complicitous and never pre-scriptive. Given this, the quiet provocation in Merleau-Ponty's Vision is the invitation to practice politics differently: how to effectively instrumentalize a critique of instrumentality, how to explain inequity and oppression without reinforcing their terms of reference, how to appreciate that puzzles about "the enigma of woman" have universal application? Feminism certainly forfeits its coherence in this re-Visioning, but hasn't it always been the case that feminism's identity is fraught with its own undoing, its own impropriety and willful curiosity about things it has previously come to accept?

If we take seriously Barad's earlier representation, namely, that "Bohr's central point [is] that the objects and the agencies of observation are inseparable parts of a single phenomenon" (2007, 315), and if this truly resonates with the science and drama of Merleau-Ponty's Vision—an *originary* chiasmatic structure and not something that operates between entities as is often assumed—then difference is never a simple loss or failure. Alterity, radical or otherwise, is intrinsic, an expression of the intra-ontology of Being itself. It is not another entity on the border of my being, an entity that marks the limits of my situation and what can be known from what is unknown.[3] If the limit to my situation is chiasmatically given, then "my" situation is more than local.

I will close with a suggestive evocation of what I have likened to the quantum problematic in Merleau-Ponty's Vision, again, from Françoise Dastur. She draws on ideas from Merleau-Ponty's essay "Eye and Mind" (1964), where he considers the fractured sense of temporality in Cézanne's paintings. Dastur quotes Merleau-Ponty's description of Vision as " 'the means given me for being absent from myself, for taking part in the fission of Being from the inside.' " Dastur adds this gloss: "Because the enigma of vision is really the enigma of *presence*, but of a 'splintered' presence that can no longer be referred to the unity of an agency of presentation, this enigma is the mystery of *simultaneity* (OE 84/146)—the mystery of a co-existence of everything in and through distance, 'of this deflagration of being' " (2000, 41). An intra-ontology such as Merleau-Ponty offers reframes questions of ontology, epistemology, ethics, and science by radically recasting the anthropological.

Notes

Chapter One: Anthropology Diffracted

1. Einstein puzzled over the apparent communication between separate parts of a quantum system. With his colleagues Boris Podolsky and Nathan Rosen, he answered these results by assuming there were hidden variables that would, when discovered, explain the anomaly (the so-called EPR paradox, in which EPR stands for Einstein-Podolsky-Rosen). This sense that the theory was "incomplete" because the precise existence of reality appeared to conform, or be caught up in some way, with the measuring apparatus was in turn countered by John Bell in 1964. Quite simply, the EPR thesis could not reproduce the myriad predictions of quantum mechanics. Alain Aspect consolidated Bell's theorem in 1982 through an actual experiment that confirmed Bell's theorem and proved quantum non-locality. For an explanation of why these experiments represent such a powerful challenge to our understanding of reality, see the discussions in chapters 4 and 5, especially around note 9 in chapter 4 and note 8 in chapter 5.

2. Barad refers us to Ballantine 1987 for a more detailed discussion.

3. One of the anonymous manuscript readers has objected to my representation here, insisting that the following thinkers "have made extensive use of Derrida with regard to the sciences and technologies of the last two centuries." Names include Gregory Ulmer in media; Hans-Joerg Rheinberger in biology; Friedrich Kittler and Avital Ronell in technology; and M. M. J. Fischer, Donna Haraway, and Lily E. Kay in science studies. If the use of Derrida was what was at stake here, the list of names could be greatly extended. However my point is that although Derrida's work has indeed been "used" as an *analytical model* and *applied to* various objects of interest—one thinks here of the title of Gregory Ulmer's first book, *Applied Grammatology* (1984)—it is precisely this sense of

deconstruction's epistemological relevance as a model that I want to trouble and rework. I am not arguing that the ontological dimensions of these authors' arguments are simply missing, but that they are not appreciated or argued in a sufficiently robust way. I offer another meditation on this same question in a more recent article, "Original Science: Nature Deconstructing Itself," (Kirby 2010).

4. For an extended discussion of the complex puzzles that attend Saussure's notion of the sign, see the first two chapters of *Telling Flesh: The Substance of the Corporeal* (Kirby 1997). I will take up the Saussurean conundrum in the next chapter.

5. A good example of this way of thinking is evident in N. Katherine Hayles, *How We Became Posthuman: Virtual Bodies in Cybernetics, Literature and Informatics* (1999).

6. For a collection of essays, some of which address similar material about biological conversation, see Sebeok and Umiker-Sebeok 1992, especially Hoffmeyer, Emmeche, Sebeok, and Merrell.

7. Despite the title of Peter Coleman's book on the subject, *Ball Lightning: A Scientific Mystery Explained* (1998), it appears from the literature that ball lightning is a contentious subject and its account remains inconclusive. See Golde 1977; Uman 1986.

8. I decided to revisit this subject while I was making revisions because I was concerned that perhaps Martin Uman's explanation had been superseded, and indeed, that Uman was no longer regarded as a significant thinker in this field. Surprisingly, the situation appears much the same and I am even more persuaded that lightning can be read as an instantiation of the graphematic structure. Today, Uman heads up the University of Florida's Camp Blanding International Center for Lightning Research and Testing. He is the chair of the university's Department of Electrical and Computer Engineering, and his views are easily accessed via a special report on lightning that aired on Nova, a PBS Science program with accompanying website. The program opens with the fictional tale of Frankenstein's monster and the use of lightning to kick-start life. However, the program's commentator draws a comparison between life's mysterious origins and the initial conditions of lightning's own propagation. "What makes life? That's still a mystery. But interestingly . . . [it] turns out that what makes lightning is also still a mystery, in fact, it's kind of a big mystery!" Researchers remain curious because the actual power of storm lightning strikes well exceeds the local energy field in the storm cloud. Dr. Joseph Dwyer from Florida Tech comments: "Nobody has ever managed to find an electric field anywhere near that big. . . . Maybe there's something wrong with our understanding of how electrical discharges get started."

To sum up the puzzle, "If thunderclouds, even great big thunderclouds, don't have electric fields big enough to generate the giant spark that lightning actually is, where's all that energy coming from?" Researchers at this point are not reconsidering the Nature of "the field" as a division of separate polarities, the notion of "location," nor explanations that presume linear causation. Faced with the problem of finding lightning's origin they are now looking to outer space for the answer.

Is it possible to at least entertain the suggestion that the universe is, and remains, that original and expanded field whose every energy transfer confounds locality? For an accessible overview, see www.pbs.org/wgbh/nova/sciencenow/3214/02.html (accessed May 16, 2009 [orig. October 18, 2005]).

9. Examples of this type of thinking are now so abundant as to be routine. See, for example, Soper 1996 and Smith 1996 for readily accessible examples. Judith Butler's work offers one of the more sophisticated and compelling manifestations of this interpretation. See in particular *Gender Trouble: Feminism and the Subversion of Identity* (1990) and *Bodies That Matter: On the Discursive Limits of "Sex"* (1993). A more sustained interrogation of Butler's commitments appears in chapter 5.

10. I am focusing on the division between Nature and Culture and the special place accorded the human in such analyses. However, and as already touched on, even in what we might call posthermeneutic analyses of systems of information that acknowledge Nature's literacy and numeracy, informational smarts are routinely separated out from some sense of corporeal support. In such cases there is an infinite regress of the Nature/Culture division, even within Nature, because the substantive ontology of the sign is inadequately engaged.

11. See, for example, Richard Dawkins's discussion of the infinite monkey theorem in *The Blind Watchmaker: Why the Evidence of Evolution Reveals a Universe without Design* (1987).

12. For an interesting meditation on Derrida's understanding of "the Einsteinian constant" and this notion of the center, see "The Central Question" in Reilly 2006. This is an especially fascinating essay, as Reilly informs us that it was Derrida's response to Hyppolite that was cited in Alan Sokal's hoax article (1996) as an exemplification of the ignorance of postmodern thinkers. Reilly offers a more generous and informed reading of Derrida's explanation of "the Einsteinian constant." See also Arkady Plotnitsky's informative discussion of this notion of "the Einsteinian constant" (1997). Plotnitsky comments on the exchange between Hyppolite and Derrida and draws our attention to the cross-disciplinary intellectual milieu at the École Normale and Collège de France that would have informed it. He also provides a more detailed analysis of the way that Derrida's work was used and abused by both Alan Sokal (1996) and Paul R. Gross and Norman Levitt (1994) in the "science wars."

Chapter Two: Just Figures?

1. See Prag and Neave 1997, especially plates 1, 4, and 5, for facial reconstructions of these and other famous figures.

2. Richard Stanford, an artist and cultural analyst who has conducted research in an Australian city morgue, informs me that measuring facial tissue depths is an ongoing research practice. The data are routinely collected each night.

3. Richard Stanford generously provided some of these details in personal correspondence. Stanford also describes some fascinating aspects of practitioners' accounts in regard to what can and cannot be included. In field notes, he remarks: "Some aspects of facial embellishment, especially those not known e.g. color of eyes, would not be included because it will detract from the purpose of recognition. . . . [However] this stage of the reconstruction revealed a complex interplay between the abstract, the real and the ideal. Discussions about the face were framed within a context of 'expert' evidence. In other words, that each decision that was made about the reconstruction could be justified within a legal or police perspective. This is the very purpose of the project and a forensic team member would not want to ever undermine the provision of 'expert' evidence. However, some of the decisions about a face really did utilize an 'ideal' that was not necessarily based on science. The skin seems to be the organ where art and science meet. Although science has placed its primary investment below the surface, the skin changes the dynamics and scope of the reconstruction. It was only during this part of the process when my questions were not always welcomed, and I detected a real edge to every conversation. I think this is the place where scientists do have to fall back on their own reflection in one form or another. There are several examples of this—they gave nicknames to every reconstruction they did; the hair on one reconstruction was styled by the same hairdresser that did the team member's hair; and in a conversation about the work of a forensic anatomist in another country, one of the team commented 'all her reconstructions just look like her' " (personal correspondence, July 11, 2001).

4. Although my argument suggests that a precise resemblance can be extruded from the data, comparisons between successful clay composites and photographs of the deceased may not reveal a likeness to someone who does not already know the person. I certainly found myself searching unsuccessfully for a "match" in what Prag and Neave were offering as a clear illustration of common identity. See the photographic comparisons for evidence of this (Prag and Neave 1997, 9 and 11). Perhaps we should regard identity as a sort of "shimmering" of expressions, where even one face involves a field of possibilities that are more or less "itself." Indeed, implied in the previous note ("all her reconstructions just look like her") is the suggestion that a person's facial landscape might retain something of its

special signature even through such apparently foreign resemblances. On this same point, Jim Swan has pointed out to me that even with photographs we concede a wide range of likenesses for one face yet make discriminations between them about how well they've captured someone's "essence." This phenomenon could also be likened to the kinesis of a moiré, or interference pattern.

5. When I originally trialed the development of this material in preliminary form at various forums, someone invariably referred me to Michael Ondaatje's *Anil's Ghost* (2000) for further insight into the mystery of facial reconstruction and recognition. Ondaatje's novel personifies the surreal nature of Sri Lankan politics from the mid-1980s to the early 1990s, where human identity could dissolve in the violent treachery of night-time acts, washing up in piles of unrecognizable debris by the sides of roads or in shallow graves. As the novel plots an attempt to "give a face" to just one of these victims, its relevance is obvious.

What strikes me as curious, however, since the book's endnote acknowledgments attest that Ondaatje has clearly done his homework on forensic facial reconstruction, is that he makes no mention of the science involved in cracking such mysteries. Rather than include the creative clairvoyance of this "arithmography," Ondaatje attributes the face's prophetic possibility to the implied spiritual capacity and prodigious artistic talents of its sculptor. This man's traditional vocation, inherited down through the centuries, is to paint the Buddha's eyes, albeit backward, by way of a mirror. In other words, he is a spiritual medium who is "in touch" with the mystery of things unseen. We are surely used to thinking about the gift of artistic talent in this way, a way that emphasizes and even identifies the specialness of creative inspiration by defining it against scientific rationalism and a rather lean sense of determinacy. What changes, however, if we open the rigidity of our concept of "determination" and "number" to the motivations we more comfortably describe as spiritual or artistic? The point here is that Ondaatje has made a quite deliberate decision to censor information that does not reinforce his view about the content and location of "artistic inspiration" and spirituality. But can we assume, as Ondaatje does despite evidence that should give him pause, that there are two quite distinct "systems" of production at work here?

6. In a much later interview, Derrida notes that the historicity of ideal objects and their representation in language is the pivotal concern of his introduction to *Origin of Geometry* and an enduring question throughout his work. See "The Time of a Thesis: Punctuations" (1983, 39).

7. This is a salutary moment to note how the ambiguations of Derridean neologisms such as "non-originary origin," "supplementary origin," or "always/already not yet" might be recast. For example, it is now received wisdom in critical

theory that when we search for an origin we inevitably discover contemporary preconceptions and desires in the nature of its identity. The reason is obvious, namely, our *re*-presentations of an irretrievable moment in time have been made to stand in for its absent identity. Unfortunately, the counterintuitive charge in Derrida's vision is considerably diluted in this return to representationalism, a return that explains away the puzzle and mystery of how apparently separate things are, on closer inspection, substantively caught up with each other. If the most challenging implications of deconstruction address the nature of identity and the conceptual apparatus that holds it in place, then time must also be subject to this reconsideration. For example, a notion of identity as an autonomous and discrete "something" is preserved if we simply divide time into an unfolding of isolated moments, moments that are necessary to the linear logic of causality, unidirectional efficacy, and the notion of difference as separation. However, if the ontology of time is internally entangled, if it is an enduring deferral/referral to itself, then discovering the present in the past is not a sign of hermetic enclosure and retrospective projection—a mistake—but something considerably more complex.

8. This point reminds us of Jean Hyppolite's assumption, expressed toward the end of the previous chapter, that the genesis of man must be an unwitting by-product, a "mutant," of Nature's scribbling. To suggest anything else would be to assume that intention, agency, and intellectual capacity (writing) preceded its arrival as what demarcates the specificity of human identity.

9. I realize that the analogy's success is qualified because we have focused on an entity, namely, one person whose very existence is unique and individual. If we begin and end with this atomic entity, then we would be forced to grant that the athlete's energies, or the original conditions that obtained at the starting line, would be depleted by the end of the race and dispersed outside her body. Or, that the taking in of oxygen would be an energy supplement not present at the beginning. However, if we think "the system" in its generalization, and don't begin by presuming to truly segregate an origin from an outside, then energy is not so much lost as it is in flux.

10. In anticipation of the argument that is about to unfold, this is a good place to mention Gödel's incompleteness theorem. The Czech mathematician Kurt Gödel is well known for demonstrating that the rules and axioms of any system of formal logic are incapable of verifying all its propositions. In other words, the system cannot understand itself in its own terms; it must refer to other systems in order to grasp or comprehend itself. Not surprisingly, the theorem is deployed more generally to explain the elusive nature of truth and the local and limited nature of knowledge, and we can see that such a reading could affirm Derrida's own convictions in the case under discussion.

Against this notion of a partial or contained knowledge we can read Derrida against himself here in order to complicate this limitation. Derrida makes positive reference to Gödel's theorem and the mathematician's notion of "undecidability" in "The Double Session," noting, "An undecidable proposition, as Gödel demonstrated in 1931, is a proposition which, given a system of axioms governing a multiplicity, is neither an analytical nor deductive consequence of those axioms, nor in contradiction with them, neither true nor false with respect to those axioms. *Tertium datur*, without synthesis" (1981a, 219).

Importantly, Mark C. Taylor argues that Derrida's appropriation of Gödel's theorem isn't a simple affirmation that marks "the unavoidable limits of human certainty and the inevitable incompleteness of all apparently complete and consistent systems" (2001, 96). Taylor refers us to a later interview in *Positions*, where Derrida dilates on the "undecidable" in a way that Taylor will argue "subtly shifts its meaning in order to expand its significance" (2001, 96). Derrida explains, "I have called undecidables, that is, unities of simulacrum, 'false' verbal properties (nominal or semantic) that can no longer be included within philosophical (binary) opposition, but which, however, inhabit philosophical opposition, resisting and disorganizing it, *without ever* constituting a third term, without ever leaving room for a solution in the form of speculative dialectics" (1981b, 43).

Taylor's aim is to underline the comprehensive complexity of an "inside," a complexity without omission. Undecidability does not imply that something is missing, for as Taylor argues, "In Derrida's reworking of Gödel's theorem, every system or structure includes as a condition of its own possibility something it cannot assimilate. This 'outside,' which is 'inside,' exposes the openness of every system that seems to be closed. Unlike the exteriority [Niklas] Luhmann attributes to autopoietic systems, this openness is not extraneous but is '*within*' the system itself" (2001, 97).

11. Even discussions of posthumanism very often recommit to the familiar frame of a substance versus information (matter versus form) split. Although the body is seen to incorporate information processing, the presumption that there is always some "substance" or "stuff" that bears (and is not) this processing is rarely interrogated. As noted in the previous chapter, for a good example of this style of thinking, see N. Katherine Hayles, *How We Became Posthuman* (1999).

12. Louise Burchill has pointed out to me that at this stage of my argument, the difference between anagrammatology and grammatology is perhaps no difference at all.

13. I should note in passing that this recuperation of the word "re-presentation" is not a return to representationalism's happy divide between two separate entities, namely, reality and the signs thought to substitute for it. Although a sense of difference is certainly being evoked here, it carries the rather extra-

ordinary sense of not being able to take its measure, its distance, from anything. Originary *différance* motors identity formation, such that entities of whatever sort are born of/through this process and do not preexist it.

Chapter Three: Enumerating Language

1. This phrase is the title of a well-known paper by the physicist Eugene P. Wigner, "The Unreasonable Effectiveness of Mathematics in the Natural Sciences" (1960).

2. Brian Rotman is a prodigious and important contributor to this field. See also *Ad Infinitum: The Ghost in Turing's Machine—Taking God Out of Mathematics and Putting the Body Back In* (1993a); *Signifying Nothing: The Semiotics of Zero* (1993b); *Mathematics as Sign* (2000).

3. This is not to discount the contribution of thinkers from both the humanities and the sciences who explore these differences and the tensions they generate. See, for example, the other essays in Barbara Herrnstein Smith and Arkady Plotnitsky, eds., *Mathematics, Science, and Postclassical Theory* (1997). Nevertheless, these studies often remain caught in debates about epistemology, only sometimes exploring more radical questions about the ontological implications of scientific and mathematical (representational) objects. For example, an article by Bruno Latour that recognizes the increasing autism of the constructivist legacy never questions the assumption that Culture mediates (turns into language and therefore transforms) the substantive facticity of Nature. Looking for clear air so that constructivism can continue to fly, Latour's conflation of deconstruction with destruction locates the latter's acid-bath analysis as the problem and his own brand of pragmatically respectful and "progressive" constructivism as the solution. Latour's stated anxiety that in deconstruction's hands the very notion of construction might exceed human definition marks a conceptual impasse that my own intervention will take up in more detail in chapter 4. See Latour, "The Promises of Constructivism" (2003).

4. For example, Rotman notes the collective efforts of Marshall McLuhan, Walter Ong, Roy Harris, and Jacques Derrida, who all argue against "the subordination of graphics to phonetics" (1997, 17). However, any assumption that these writers represent a united effort in this direction is quite misleading. Ong's argument, for example, links orality to an original primitivism of emotional and perceptual immediacy. Not surprisingly, these affinities are compared to literate Cultures where the technologization of the word is associated with more abstract forms of thinking, assumed to be less reliant upon experience and the physical world for their functionality. Derrida's intervention into the speech/writing prob-

lematic challenges such representations, as well as the evaluations that underpin their linear evolution from the concrete to the ideationally complex (from body to mind, Nature to Culture, immediate to mediated). If so-called oral peoples are able to read the country, perceive its grammar, and communicate and represent its regulative rhythms to each other in different media, how is this different from the abstractions Ong attributes to literacy? Ong's inability to detect an alphabet or its legible equivalent leads him to conclude that writing is absent, just as Claude Lévi-Strauss assumed that the wavy lines and scratchings of the Nambikwara on their calabashes were the sad (and meaningless) imitations of writing proper. For an elaboration of these different positions see Ong 1982 and Derrida 1984.

5. For a contemporary representation and extended explanation of the view that mathematics is discovered and not invented because it is "absolute, universal, and therefore independent of any cultural influence" (5), see Changeux and Connes 1995. Interestingly, the complication of Connes's commitment to a "preexisiting mathematical world that is logically prior to any human intervention" (1995, 89) comes in its radical displacement of the conventional coordinates through which we normally conceptualize the *physis/thesis* division. Not only is the role of the human dispensed with as the origin of invention and abstraction, but the materiality of physical Nature also seems irrelevant. As Connes insists, "The idea that mathematical reality is located in the physical world is foreign to my way of thinking" (1995, 47). Understandably, Connes's Platonic commitments, with their accompanying denials, become the focus of Changeux's irritation, just as the specific erasure of physical experience also concentrates Rotman's interventionary impulse. However, if the direction of Changeux's argument seems productive because it implicitly queries the identity of mathematics by acknowledging its corporeal situation, there is something peculiarly destabilizing and confronting in Connes's mathematical utopia, this *no place* that might nevertheless complicate Changeux's humanism and the routine of its logic. Although the positions of Changeux and Connes often appear as irreconcilable caricatures of this question's difficulties, my own argument will attempt to reassess the apparent opposition in their perspectives.

6. It could be said that Rotman and I do not assess the influence of typeset mathematical and alphabetic production for our respective arguments, in other words, the legible effects of mundane machines. Although this question may have some purchase for Rotman's concerns—and it certainly has its place—it can also operate to obscure more general questions about the very ontology of language, what it is and how it works. To this end, since my inquiry into the notion of "script" and "writing" asks why it isn't generalized to include such things as neuronal, pheromonal, and even chemical communication, its specific mechanical reproduction is of little consequence to this particular inquiry.

7. As mentioned in chapter 3, "spooky action at a distance" captured Einstein's disbelief in what appeared to be the "nonlocal" behaviors of apparently independent phenomena. Einstein's assumption that missing information would resolve the puzzle and reinstall a more classical explanation of the workings of the universe (in terms of identity and causality) is now regarded as quite misguided after Alain Aspect's experiments in 1982. See Nadeau and Kafatos, *The Non-Local Universe: The New Physics and Matters of the Mind* (2001). The quantum problematic will be taken up briefly in chapter 4, and in more extended discussion in chapter 6.

8. We see a clear illustration of this point in Michel Foucault's intervention into the Marxist legacy that divided base from superstructure and matter from ideality. Foucault's work provides us with an opportunity to rethink the substance versus form (Nature as opposed to Culture) divisions because he insists that discursive formations do not seize upon bodies that preexist those formations. There are many ways to interpret this elision of an origin, and the most comfortable option is to assume that the origin preexists, and therefore eludes, accurate representation. However, if the truth of pleasures and sexualities mutates and transforms across time and space such that the body is not a fixed origin or stable reference point, then we must surely wonder about biology's capacity to enact this lived plasticity. How does biology reconfigure itself—its erogenous zones, its hormonal expressions, its neuronal activity—according to the mutations of these different scripts? Unfortunately, this last question has been buried under "cultural constructionist" arguments that interpret appeals to biology or Nature as conservative and misguided. The insistence that everything is a "discursive construction" has too readily assumed that "language" and "inscription" are synonymous with "Culture."

9. In the last chapter of *Telling Flesh: The Substance of the Corporeal* (1997), I address the broader relevance of Derrida's work and invite readers to challenge its disciplinary confinement. See also Kirby 1999 and especially Johnson 1993.

10. Karen Barad has pointed out to me that what I assumed was just a random example, in this case a triangle, was a telling choice, as "Δ" is "delta" in the Greek alphabet, a sign that would have been spoken.

Not unrelated is the example of Saussure's famous diagram of the tree and the horse with Latin words next to them. Whenever I ask a class to look at the page and nominate which is the signifier and which is the signified, there is almost (if not always) unanimous voting for the illustration as the signified. Their justifications are that the word is abstract, the image is not, because the image is real, or more real. If I suggest that the word is also an image, that it is a diagram, that it is as concrete or abstract as the illustration because it is also an illustration the students seem all at sea. Even in the telling of this little experiment I am forced to anticipate a logic that has been naturalized, as Rotman rightly points out.

11. Regarding the resonating implosion, or grammatology of ~~the~~ "gram," Derrida has some helpful comments. In *Of Grammatology* he notes Saussure's failure to explain how writing can be an "image" of the phoneme, a "figuration" or "representation" of language, if language and writing are "two distinct systems of signs" (1984, 45). Derrida evokes Freud's discussion of the dreamwork's condensations and the knot/not of its accumulated contradictions and ironic juxtapositions to illuminate Saussure's apparent "satisfaction" with his definitions. After all, what else could Saussure do with these thoughts that, when put together, contravene the grounding assumptions of the linguistic tradition he inherited and continued to work within. As Derrida explains, "In fact, even within so-called phonetic writing, the 'graphic' signifier refers to the phoneme through a web of many dimensions which *binds* it, like all signifiers, to other written and oral signifiers, within a 'total' system open, let us say, to all possible investments of sense. We must begin with the possibility of that total system" (1984, 45; my emphasis).

A further elucidation of "all the investitures to which a *graphie*, in form and substance, is submitted" (1984, 87) comes in the rather charming discussion of Melanie Klein's young patient, Fritz. Derrida cites Klein's case notes in order to at least begin to announce the graphematic webbing, or systemic totality, that is already alive in any linguistic "unit." Klein throughout underlines the psychoanalytic return to sexuality as the final/original explanation of these fantasies, and we would need to interrogate this further. However, for our purposes here, Klein's notes exemplify the impossibility of a single, isolated atom of meaning. We witness this in her discussion of the cinematic reverie that informs an apparently lone letter, discovering within it a bildungsroman of epic proportion: "For Fritz, when he was *writing,* the lines meant roads and the letters ride on motor-bicycles —on the pen—upon them. For instance, 'i' and 'e' ride together on a motor-bicycle that is usually driven by the 'i' and they love one another with a tenderness quite unknown in the real world. . . . The 'i's are skillful, distinguished and clever, have many pointed weapons, and live in caves, between which, however, there are also mountains, gardens and harbours. . . . On the other hand, the '1's are represented as stupid, clumsy, lazy and dirty. They live in caves under the earth" (Klein in Derrida, 1984, 333).

Derrida goes on to use this, as well as similar evidence, to illustrate that the difference between the multiple layers of signification *within* Chinese picture-script compared with the single registration of an alphabetic letter may be no difference at all. Klein notes that for every individual child each letter is pregnant with phantasies whose "condensation, displacement and other mechanisms [are] familiar to us from dreams and neuroses" (in Derrida 1984, 334). Although the following is a rather long quotation, it exemplifies, albeit in preliminary form, how congested the webbing of any "one" gram must be: "It can be observed how the sexual-symbolic meaning of the penholder merges into the act of writing that the latter discharges. In the same way, the libidinal significance of reading is derived from the symbolic cathexis of the book and the eye. In this there are at work, of course, also other determinants afforded by the component instincts, such as 'peeping' in reading, and exhibitionistic, aggressive sadistic tendencies in writing; at the root of the sexual-symbolic meaning of the penholder lay probably originally that of the weapon and the hand. Corresponding with this too the activity of reading is a more passive, that of writing a more active, one, and for the inhibitions of one or the other of them the various fixations on the pregenital stages of organization are also significant" (Klein in Derrida 1984, 334).

12. This debate was introduced in note 5.

Chapter Four: Natural Convers(at)ions

1. A system theorist such as Niklas Luhmann (1995; 2002), for example, presumes the integrity of different systems and identifies them accordingly. For Luhmann, there is an inside and an outside of any particular system. Although a system has an environment that functions at its boundaries, each system exists in its own right, even though it can be open to conversation with other systems in its purview. Similarly, the biologists Humberto Maturana and Francisco Varela (1992), whose writings have greatly inspired Luhmann, work with an aggregation of systems that communicate with each other. They characterize all living systems as autopoietic, that is, self-producing entities. Living systems are considered self-referential because they can only act in accordance with the demands of their own internal dynamics and regulatory states. However, Maturana and Varela also insist that as networks of communication, autopoietic entities remain open to changes, or triggers, from the environment (the outside of any particular system).

What should emerge from the following discussion is that such conceptualizations are wedded to a notion of difference as something that falls in-between identities (systems), a notion that fails to appreciate that differentiation is internal to, indeed, the very stuff of, what is evoked in the notion of systematicity. Without this appreciation we return to individual systems communicating with each other —a return to the linear logic that defines sender against receiver, and separates cause from effect. For a pathfinding and generous reading of how we might approach this work, attending to what is most provocative in its insights and furthering their implications, see Florence Chiew, "Systems Theories and Bioinformatics," forthcoming.

2. As Descartes has been positioned as something of a bad-boy, a foil against

which feminist and cultural analysis can take both leverage and distance, it seems only fair to note that readings of Descartes that destabilize this reception are also coming through. See, for example, Gaukroger 1997, Bordo 1999, Bordo and Moussa 1999, and Rodis-Lewis 1998.

3. Jacques Derrida's early work on the logic of the supplement is especially pertinent here. See Derrida 1984.

4. See Elizabeth Wilson for an interesting discussion of this phenomenon (1998, 189–98). For a more recent and accessible argument that acknowledges that changes in cultural and behavioral patterns are neurologically registered (such that we might posit that the origin or "author" of the behavior isn't Culture writing on biology, but biology writing/rewiring itself), see Norman Doidge, *The Brain That Changes Itself* (2007).

5. Jesper Hoffmeyer and Claus Emmeche are among a group of Danish biosemioticians who rely heavily on the triadic structure in Peirce's semiotic to explain biological processes. See, for example, Emmeche and Hoffmeyer 1991a, 1991b; Hoffmeyer 1996.

6. Although the point is made in passing in *Of Grammatology* (1984, 9), Derrida specifically addresses this connection in a series of seminars on the Nobel Prize winner François Jacob, who worked on the language of RNA. To date, the seminars remain unpublished (Derrida 1975).

7. Karen Barad elaborates why her use of the term "phenomena," a term she equates with ontological entanglement, is preferable to particularism—"the view that the world is composed of individuals and that each individual has its own roster of non-relational properties" (2007, 333). Such a description succinctly captures the sorts of commitments that might be heard in the broad church of poststructural thinking, even though the reasoning behind it would certainly differ.

8. As mentioned in chapter 1, experiments undertaken by John Bell in 1964 and later by Alain Aspect and, more recently, Nicolas Gisin have made empirical confirmation of nonlocality. In sum, this means that a split photon, separated from its "twin" in space (and theoretically, this can be across enormous distances), will nevertheless mirror and respond to whatever interference is applied to its "other half" as if it remains intact. Because subliminal communication is prohibited in terms of relativity, this seriously challenges our everyday notions about the world's separation into discrete objects with defined attributes that obey local causality. Consequently, if any "event" in the universe can somehow involve the broadest of distances and time frames, then we can at least entertain the possibility that the local might be articulated through, or even as, the universal and vice versa. This extraordinary suggestion compromises spatial divisions and even temporal differences: the notion of individuated events *in* time or *in* space is imploded. For a helpful introduction to this field of inquiry, see Nadeau

and Kafatos 2001, and Karen Barad's detailed and accessible unpacking of many of these provocations (2007).

9. See note 8 of chapter 5 for a further discussion of this phenomenon, especially as it manifests in John Wheeler's "delayed choice" *gedanken* (thought) experiment.

10. Science studies, like any disciplinary formation, is not a uniform set of assumptions but an evolving argument between its various practitioners and those who engage their writings. It should be noted that feminists working within the sciences have played a prominent part in establishing science studies as a specific field of interest, whether intentionally or not, and like Latour, they have brought a certain respect for scientific practices and epistemologies into dialogue with the sorts of cultural criticism that investigates the political agendas that inform them. For many critics such as Latour, cultural criticism and scientific research need not be positioned in an agonistic way. Among prominent thinkers who originally hail from the sciences and retain an interest in the value of its specificity, we might note Donna Haraway, Anne Fausto-Sterling, Karen Barad, Evelyn Fox Keller, Susan Oyama, and Elizabeth Wilson.

11. Although Latour's enthusiasm for the value of ANT has faded in more recent writings, his work continues to tease out many of the questions it raises. For an early example of this style of thinking, see Latour 1993a. Other notable thinkers in the field of actor-network theory include Michael Callon, John Law, M. Lynch, Steve Woolgar, and S. L. Star.

12. On the need to develop a more generous critical practice, see Butler 2001 and Latour 2004a.

Chapter Five: (Con)founding "the Human"

1. It is important to appreciate that claims about the unreliability of observation and memory are not unique to postmodern and poststructural criticism. Empirical research on eyewitness testimony, for example, shows that details of a crime scene, such as facial recognition, the description, or even existence of important objects at the scene, and the narrative timing and content of events, are notoriously plastic. The recollections of witnesses can be manipulated by suggestion, whether intentional or inadvertent. This predicament attends all acts of memory. See, for example, Hall, Loftus, and Tousignant 1984 and Wells 1984.

2. The terms "patternment" and "points in the pattern" were favored by the linguist Edward Sapir as a gloss for significance and taken up by his student and later collaborator, Benjamin Lee Whorf. What is interesting about the terms is the way they capture something fascinating in the very process of recognition,

namely, how does a gestalt have functional purchase, given that other languages will recognize different "points in the pattern"? I have always liked the term "patternment," as it refuses nominalist assumptions that derive meaning from reference. "Patternment" asks *how* the apparent bond between a sign and what appears to be a functioning referent actually arises. The relevance of these early precursors to the question at hand is evident in the debates they have generated about the nature of reality and the effective practice of science. See Sapir 1925 and 1927, and Whorf 1956.

3. See Morris, *The Culture of Pain* (1991), for an interesting overview of this point.

4. A long history of feminist criticism and intervention, for example, takes its leverage from this insight and elaborates the conservative investments in, but also the necessary reliance upon, naturalizing arguments. I am thinking here of such influential writers as Simone de Beauvoir, Diana Fuss, Jane Gallop, Elizabeth Grosz, Hélène Cixous—another fifty names and we would still be at the beginning of this list of acknowledgments. The intricacies and paradoxes in these same arguments reveal just how slippery a referent can be, even a referent with the palpability and sensual immediacy of the body. The following meditation explores this enduring puzzle and suggests that the most unthinkable and yet radical assault on prejudice is to return to Nature its explanatory and constitutive powers.

5. Butler's understanding of the "chiasm," a term whose special associations with Maurice Merleau-Ponty will be explored in the next chapter, is evident here. It could be likened to a constitutive interference or "interactivity," an operation *between* entities; here, Nature *and* Culture. Importantly, as we will see, it is not an originary entanglement that produces the entities as different forms of the one phenomenon.

6. As we saw in the previous chapter, writers such as Bruno Latour express impatience with the postmodern privileging of Culture and the resulting evacuation and erasure of Nature from critical analysis. However, although Latour's solution includes Nature in the *dispositif* of power that forges a referent, he rather vigilantly maintains the difference between Nature and Culture. Latour does concede that Nature has language, but it is confined to the babble of speech: it seems that only humans can abstract—read, interpret, and cogitate. While Latour's speech/writing split cannot be sustained, for even speech is a mediated abstraction, Latour's work does very often capture the sheer wonder of the Nature/Culture problematic and why this division is untenable. See especially Latour 1999 and 2004c.

7. See Barad's discussion of performativity and her engagement with the weakness in Butler's position (2007, 59–65). Barad goes on to reconfigure perfor-

mativity as "agential realism," a notion that embraces the philosophy-physics of Niels Bohr. The relevance of these quantum themes will be taken up again in the final chapter.

8. See note 9 in chapter 4, which makes mention of these experiments. Especially provocative is John Wheeler's "delayed choice thought experiment," which suggests that if the quantum resonance between the observer's choice and the observed phenomenon's "compliance" *across space* is accepted, then the distinction between separate "moments" or "events" *in time* must also collapse. This would mean that decisions made in the present could, at least theoretically, determine the course of past reality "in no time," or more frustratingly, it would undo the very coordinates of the question's narrative presumption. And this appears to be the case. It would also destabilize any sense that the decision to undertake the experiment can be attributed to a specific locus, or entity—the human. The spatial separations of causality, at least in the presumption of a single origin of influence and efficacy, will not hold in quantum explanations.

Following this, what we are to make of nonlocality, despite its overwhelming acceptance in the scientific community, remains contested. Paul Davies, for example, comments, "The world is not a collection of separate but coupled *things*; rather it is a network of *relations*" (1983, 112). Davies quotes Werner Heisenberg to affirm this puzzle: "The common division of the world into subject and object, inner world and outer world, body and soul is no longer adequate" (112). And yet despite this, Heisenberg's commitments (which might be likened to Butler's understanding of interference) and those of Niels Bohr are incongruent and at loggerheads, as Karen Barad makes clear (2007, 294–302). Same words, different worlds.

9. A cluster of texts that will introduce the humanities reader to the literary or textual nature of biology, a textuality that provokes us to ask "who" writes this text, includes Freud 1961, and Jacques Derrida's thoughtful response to it (1985), as well as Wilson 1998. The more recognizable field of biosemiotics, which draws on the work of Charles Sanders Peirce, is also helpful here. See, for example, the collection of essays in Sebeok and Umiker-Sebeok 1992, and Wheeler 2006. A path-finding elaboration of Jacques Derrida's "general text" can be found in Johnson 1993, which also directs the reader to the cybernetic implications of code.

10. An earlier version of the following argument appears in Kirby 2006.

11. See, for example, Morris 1991 and Greco 1998.

12. Elizabeth Wilson has informed me that some psychoanalysts, building on recent evidence in infant development, contend there is some kind of primordial, or proto-self much earlier than Lacan's mirror-stage. As she explains, "What makes these recent developments interesting, from the point of view of the argument being made here, is that this pre-mirror stage self is not considered

Cartesian in the way Lacan critiques, but rather an open system of affective, motor, perceptual inter-courses with parent and world" (personal correspondence). See Stern 2000, and the recent empirical work of Peter Fonagy et al. (2005).

13. The reference to "Bisexuality" in Laplanche and Pontalis, *The Language of Psychoanalysis* (1973), is helpful here.

14. In previous chapters we have noted the importance of the term "consubstantial" to Ferdinand de Saussure's description of the sign's paradoxical identity —an "entity" whose invariance is made possible by a system of referral that is pure variation. It is important to recognize that the many contradictions in Saussure's text witness an inability to resolve the notion of reference and to analyze the sign's purported identity and internal differences in terms of separate and different functions and attributions.

15. For an inspiring essay on the question of power as an originary force, a natural and normative force whose performative outcomes need not rest on failure, see Pierre Macherey's "Towards a Natural History of Norms" (1992). Lee Edelman's *No Future* (2004) is also relevant here, as it encourages us to refuse those political and social structures whose reproductive futurity promise more of the same. His call to embrace the negative, to take a risk, has parallels in my own argument's call to biologize the unnatural and refuse a politics based in Culture's redemptive promise.

Chapter Six: Culpability and the Double-Cross

1. I use the word "ecology" suggestively and heuristically at this stage of the argument. It is not meant to evoke, for example, a style of thinking such as James Lovelock's sense of Gaia—one living world of interlocking parts and functions— nor a sense of benign possibility about acknowledging the human debt to the natural world. For example, Moniker Langer, in "Merleau-Ponty and Deep Ecology," comments: "For Merleau-Ponty, self and nonself, human and nonhuman, intertwine in a mutual enfolding, such that comprehension itself becomes a relation of 'embrace' with the other" (1990, 115). As the current state of the world is already a result of what Langer describes, the moral sense of good that the word "embrace" effects, as well as the presumption that different (preexisting) entities come together in this embrace (which is not *already* the very stuff of their "individual" ontological possibility), overlooks the more radical implications of what we might call Merleau-Ponty's "intra-ontology."

2. Although there are many different readings of quantum complexity, the conclusion that Einstein was incorrect in his assumption that hidden variables

would be found to explain the nonlocality paradox and return us to a classical understanding of the universe (isolates, causality, etc.) that reflected common-sense is now generally conceded. See the brief explanation of Einstein's position in chapter 1, note 1.

3. Time prevents me from exploring the relevance of Emmanual Levinas to this debate. For an excellent analysis of why the Levinasian notion of the ethical relation "in which the Other remains transcendent, irreducibly different, 'forever unknowable' " (2006, 261) is incompatible with Merleau-Ponty's understanding of a chiasmatic ontology, see Ann V. Murphy's "Language in the Flesh: The Politics of Discourse in Merleau-Ponty, Levinas, and Irigaray" (2006).

Following a path not unrelated to the figuring of this question in terms of limits—exceeding them, falling short of them, knowing some things, but then confronting an outside of knowledge, an ineffable—I have relied on Barad's reading of quantum physics rather than those of the only other person who is well known in critical theory circles for his work in this field, Arkady Plotnitsky. Although his work is certainly erudite and well argued, I am in disagreement with its basic premise. For example, in the preface to *The Knowable and the Unknowable: Modern Science, Nonclassical Thought, and the "Two Cultures"* (2005), he explains the importance of quantum mechanics and nonclassical theories: "This thinking and these theories radically redefine the nature of knowledge by making the unknowable an irreducible part of knowledge, insofar as the ultimate objects under investigation by nonclassical theories are seen as being beyond any knowledge or even conception, while, at the same time, affecting what is knowable" (2005, xiii). I am more interested in a reading of the chiasm (and indeed, Derrida's *différance*) as a generalized dehiscence—an ontologizing that includes (and therefore fractures) the limit and redefines reference, and science, altogether. The installation of a limit that is not itself subject to this fracturing derives from a very different, indeed, classical understanding of language/system, where difference is understood in terms of assemblage, and making a difference is having the capacity to interfere.

Works Cited

Ballantine, F. J. 1987. "Resource Letter Iqm-2: Foundations of Quantum Mechanics since the Bell Inequalities." *American Journal of Physics* 55:785–92.

Barad, Karen. 2007. *Meeting the Universe Halfway: Quantum Physics and the Entanglement of Matter and Meaning*. Durham: Duke University Press.

Bernet, Rudolf. 1989. "On Derrida's 'Introduction' to Husserl's *Origin of Geometry*." In *Derrida and Deconstruction*, edited by Hugh Silverman. New York: Routledge.

Bordo, Susan. 1999. "Introduction." In *Feminist Interpretations of René Descartes*, edited by Susan Bordo. University Park: Pennsylvania State University Press.

Bordo, Susan, and Mario Moussa. 1999. "Rehabilitating the 'I.'" In *Feminist Interpretations of René Descartes*, edited by Susan Bordo. University Park: Pennsylvania State University Press.

Breen, Margaret Soenser, et al. 2001. "'There Is a Person Here': An Interview with Judith Butler." *International Journal of Sexuality and Gender Studies* 6 (nos. 1–2): 7–23.

Burke, Carolyn. 1981. "Irigaray through the Looking Glass." *Feminist Studies* 7 (2)(Summer): 288–306.

Butler, Judith. 1990. *Gender Trouble: Feminism and the Subversion of Identity*. New York: Routledge.

———. 1993. *Bodies That Matter: On the Discursive Limits of "Sex."* New York: Routledge.

———. 2001. "What Is Critique?: An Essay on Foucault's Virtue." In *The Political*, edited by David Ingram. Oxford: Blackwell.

Changeux, Jean-Pierre, and Alain Connes. 1995. *Conversations on Mind, Matter, and Mathematics*, edited and translated by M. B. DeBevoise. Princeton: Princeton University Press.

Chanter, Tina. 2000. "Wild Meaning: Luce Irigaray's Reading of Merleau-Ponty." In *Chiasms: Merleau-Ponty's Notion of Flesh*, edited by Fred Evans and Leonard Lawlor. Albany: State University of New York Press.

Chiew, Florence. "Systems Theories and Bioinformatics," PhD dissertation. In Progress. University of New South Wales, Sydney.

Coleman, Peter. F. 1998. *Ball Lightning: A Scientific Mystery Explained*. Christchurch, New Zealand: Fireshine Press.

Dastur, Françoise. 2000. "World, Flesh, Vision." In *Chiasms: Merleau-Ponty's Notion of Flesh*, edited by Fred Evans and Leonard Lawlor. Albany: State University of New York Press.

Davies, Paul. 1983. *God and the New Physics*. New York: Simon and Schuster.

Dawkins, Richard. 1987. *The Blind Watchmaker: Why the Evidence of Evolution Reveals a Universe without Design*. Norton: New York.

Derrida, Jacques. 1970. "Structure, Sign, and Play in the Discourse of the Human Sciences" and "Discussion." In *The Languages of Criticism and the Sciences of Man: The Structuralist Controversy*, edited by R. Macksey and E. Donato. Baltimore: Johns Hopkins University Press.

——. 1975. *La Vie La Mort*, translated by Antonia Pont. Jacques Derrida Papers, MS-CO1, Special Collections and Archives, University of California–Irvine Libraries, Irvine.

——. 1981a. "The Double Session" [1972]. In *Dissemination*, translated by Barbara Johnson. Chicago: University of Chicago Press.

——. 1981b. *Positions* [1972]. Translated by Alan Bass. Chicago: University of Chicago Press.

——. 1983. "The Time of a Thesis: Punctuations." In *Philosophy in France Today*, edited by A. Montefiore. Cambridge: Cambridge University Press.

——. 1984. *Of Grammatology* [1974]. Translated by G. C. Spivak. Baltimore: Johns Hopkins University Press.

——. 1985. "Freud and the Scene of Writing." In *Writing and Difference*, translated by Alan Bass. London: Routledge and Kegan Paul.

——. 1988. "Afterword: Toward an Ethic of Discussion." In *Limited INC*, translated by S. Weber. Evanston: Northwestern University Press.

——. 1989. *Edmund Husserl's Origin of Geometry: An Introduction* [1962]. Translated by J. P. Leavey Jr. Lincoln: University of Nebraska Press.

——. 2001. "As If it Were Possible, 'Within Such Limits.' " In *Questioning Derrida: With His Replies on Philosophy*, edited by M. Meyer. Aldershot, U.K.: Ashgate.

——. 2002. "The Animal That Therefore I Am (More to Follow)." Translated by David Wills. *Critical Inquiry* 28 (2): 369–418.

——. 2003. "And Say the Animal Responded?" In *Zoontologies: The Question of the Animal*, edited by Cary Wolfe, translated by David Wills. Minneapolis: University of Minnesota Press.

Derrida, Jacques, and Geoffrey Bennington. 1993. *Jacques Derrida*. Translated by Geoffrey Bennington. Chicago: University of Chicago Press.

Devlin, Keith. 2000. *The Maths Gene*. London: Weidenfeld and Nicolson.

Doidge, Norman. 2007. *The Brain That Changes Itself*. Melbourne, Australia: Scribe.

Edelman, Lee. 2004. *No Future: Queer Theory and the Death Drive*. Durham: Duke University Press.

Emmeche, Claus, and Jesper Hoffmeyer. 1991a. "Code-duality and the Semiotics of Nature." In *On Semiotic Modelling*, edited by M. Anderson and F. Merrel. Berlin: Mouton de Gruyter.

———. 1991b. "From Language to Nature: The Semiotic Metaphor in Biology." *Semiotica* 84 (1–2): 1–42.

Fonagy, Peter., et al. 2005. *The Interpersonal World of the Infant: A View from Psychoanalysis and Developmental Psychology*. New York: Other Press.

Foucault, Michel. 1980. *The History of Sexuality, Volume 1: An Introduction*. Translated by Robert Hurley. New York: Vintage Books.

Freud, Sigmund. 1961. "A Note upon the Mystic Writing Pad." In *Standard Edition of the Complete Psychological Works of Sigmund Freud*, vol. 19, edited by J. Strachey. London: Hogarth Press.

Gadet, Françoise. 1989. *Saussure and Contemporary Culture*. Translated by G. Elliott. London: Hutchinson Radius.

Gasché, Rodolphe. 1986. *The Tain of the Mirror: Derrida and the Philosophy of Reflection*. Cambridge: Harvard University Press.

Gaukroger, Stephen. 1997. "Nature without Reason: Cartesian Automata and Perceptual Cognition." In *The Genealogy of Knowledge: Analytical Essays in the History and Philosophy of Science*, edited by S. Gaukroger. Sydney, Australia: Ashgate.

Golde, Rudolf H. 1977. *Lightning: Physics of Lightning*, vol. 1. New York: Academic Press.

Greco, Monica. 1998. *Illness as a Work of Thought: A Foucauldian Perspective on Psychosomatics*. London: Routledge.

Gross, Paul R., and Norman Levitt. 1994. *Higher Superstition: The Academic Left and its Quarrels with Science*. Baltimore: Johns Hopkins University Press.

Hall, D. F., E. L. Loftus, and J. P. Tousignant. 1984. "Post-Event Information and Changes in Recollection for a Natural Event." In *Eyewitness Testimony: Psychological Perspectives*, edited by G. L. Wells and E. F. Loftus. Cambridge: Cambridge University Press.

Hayles, N. Katherine. 1999. *How We Became Posthuman: Virtual Bodies in Cybernetics, Literature and Informatics*. Chicago: University of Chicago Press.

Hoffmeyer, Jesper. 1996. *Signs of Meaning in the Universe*, translated by B. J. Haveland. Bloomington: Indiana University Press.

Irigaray, Luce. 1985a. *Speculum of the Other Woman*. Translated by G. C. Gill. Ithaca: Cornell University Press.

——. 1985b. *This Sex Which Is Not One*. Translated by C. Porter with C. Burke. Ithaca: Cornell University Press.

——. 1993. *An Ethics of Sexual Difference*. Translated by C. Burke and G. Gill. Ithaca: Cornell University Press.

Johnson, Christopher. 1993. *System and Writing in the Philosophy of Jacques Derrida*. Cambridge: Cambridge University Press.

Kirby, Vicki. 1997. *Telling Flesh: The Substance of the Corporeal*. New York: Routledge.

——. 1999. "Human/Nature." *Australian Feminist Studies* 14 (29): 19–29.

——. 2006. *Judith Butler: Live Theory*. London: Continuum.

——. 2010. "Original Science: Nature Deconstructing Itself." *Derrida Today* 3 (2): 201–20.

Langer, Monika. 1990. "Merleau-Ponty and Deep Ecology." In *Ontology and Alterity in Merleau-Ponty*, edited by Galen A. Johnson and Michael B. Smith. Evanston: Northwestern University Press.

Laplanche, Jean., and J. B. Pontalis. 1973. *The Language of Psychoanalysis*, translated by D. Nicholson-Smith. New York: Norton.

Latour, Bruno. 1993a. "An Interview with Bruno Latour." Interview by T. Hugh Crawford. *Configurations: Journal of Literature, Science and Technology* 1 (2): 247–68.

——. 1993b. *We Have Never Been Modern*. Translated by Catherine Porter. Cambridge: Harvard University Press.

——. 1999. *Pandora's Hope: Essays on the Reality of Science Studies*. Cambridge: Harvard University Press.

——. 2003. "The Promises of Constructivism." In *Chasing Technoscience: Matrix for Materiality*, edited by D. Idhe and E. Selinger. Bloomington: Indiana University Press.

——. 2004a. "Interview with Bruno Latour: Decoding the Collective Experiment." Interview by Maria J. Prieto and Elise S. Youn. July 5. At http://aggluti nations.com/archives/000040.html (accessed May 16, 2009).

——. 2004b. *Politics of Nature: How to Bring the Sciences into Democracy*. Cambridge: Harvard University Press.

——. 2004c. "Why Has Critique Run Out of Steam? From Matters of Fact to Matters of Concern." *Critical Inquiry* 30 (2): 225–48.

Lotringer, Sylvère. 1973. "The Game of the Name." *diacritics* 3 (2): 2–9.

Luhmann, Niklas. 1995. *Social Systems*. Translated by John Bednarz Jr. and Dirk Baecker. Stanford: Stanford University Press.

——. 2002. *Theories of Distinction: Redescribing the Descriptions of Modernity.* Edited by William Rasch. Stanford: Stanford University Press.

Macherey, Pierre. 1992. "Towards a Natural History of Norms." In *Michel Foucault Philosopher.* New York: Routledge.

Macksey, Richard, and Eugenio Donato, eds. 1970. *The Languages of Criticism and the Sciences of Man: The Structuralist Controversy.* Baltimore: Johns Hopkins University Press.

Maturana, Humberto, and Francisco Varela. 1992. *The Tree of Knowledge.* Boston: Shambhala Publications.

Merleau-Ponty, Maurice. 1982–83. "The Experience of Others." Translated by F. Evans and H. J. Silverman. *Review of Existential Psychology and Psychiatry* 28:1–3.

——. 1962. *The Phenomenology of Perception.* Translated by C. Smith. London: Routledge and Kegan Paul.

——. 1964. "Eye and Mind." Translated by Carleton Dallery. In *The Primacy of Perception*, edited by James Edie. Evanston: Northwestern University Press, 159–90.

——. 1968. *The Visible and the Invisible.* Translated by A. Lingis. Evanston: Northwestern University Press.

——. 1995. *Signs.* Translated by R. C. McCleary. Evanston: Northwestern University Press.

Morris, D. B. 1991. *The Culture of Pain.* Berkeley: University of California Press.

Murphy, Ann V. 2006. "Language in the Flesh: The Politics of Discourse in Merleau-Ponty, Levinas, and Irigaray." In *Feminist Interpretations of Maurice Merleau-Ponty*, edited by Dorothea Olkowski and Gail Weiss. University Park: Pennsylvania State University Press.

Nadeau, Robert, and Menas Kafatos. 2001. *The Non-Local Universe: The New Physics and Matters of the Mind.* Oxford: Oxford University Press.

Norris, Christopher. 1997. "Deconstructing Anti-Realism: Quantum Mechanics and Interpretation Theory." *SubStance: A Review of Theory and Literary Criticism* 26 (3): 3–37.

Nova: Science Now. October 18, 2005. PBS website at www.pbs.org/wgbh/nova/sciencenow/3214/02.html (accessed May 16, 2009).

Ondaatje, Michael. 2000. *Anil's Ghost.* New York: Knopf.

Ong, Walter. 1982. *Orality and Literacy: The Technologizing of the Word.* London: Methuen.

Plotnitsky, Arkady. 1997. "'But It Is Above All Not True': Derrida, Relativity, and the 'Science Wars.'" *Postmodern Culture* 7 (2).

——. 2002. *The Knowable and the Unknowable: Modern Science, Nonclassical Thought, and the "Two Cultures."* Ann Arbor: University of Michigan Press.

Prag, John, and Richard Neave. 1997. *Making Faces: Using Forensic and Archae-ological Evidence*. London: British Museum Press.

Protevi, John. 2001. *Political Physics: Deleuze, Derrida and the Body Politic*. London: Athlone.

Reilly, Brian J. 2006. "Hopkins Impromptu: Following Jacques Derrida through *Theory's Empire*." *Modern Lanuage Notes* 121:911–28.

Rodis-Lewis, Genevieve. 1998. "Descartes and the Unity of the Human Being." In *Descartes*, edited by J. Cottingham. Oxford: Oxford University Press.

Rotman, Brian. 1993a. *Ad Infinitum: The Ghost in Turing's Machine—Taking God out of Mathematics and Putting the Body Back In*. Stanford: Stanford University Press.

———. 1993b. *Signifying Nothing: The Semiotics of Zero*. Stanford: Stanford University Press.

———. 1997. "Thinking Dia-Grams: Mathematics, Writing, and Virtual Reality." In *Mathematics, Science, and Postclassical Theory*, edited by Barbara Herrnstein Smith and Arkady Plotnitsky. Durham: Duke University Press.

———. 2000. *Mathematics as Sign*. Stanford: Stanford University Press.

Sapir, Edward. 1925. "Sound Patterns in Language." *Language* 1:37–51.

———. 1927. "The Unconscious Patterning of Behavior in Society." In *The Unconscious: A Symposium*, edited by E. S. Dummer. New York: Knopf.

Saussure, Ferdinand de. 1981. *Course in General Linguistics* [1916]. Edited by Charles Bally and Albert Sechehaye in collaboration with Albert Reidlinger, translated by Wade Baskin. Bungay, U.K.: Fontana/Collins.

Sebeok, T. A., and J. Umiker-Sebeok, eds. 1992. *Biosemiotics: The Semiotic Web 1991*. Berlin: Mouton de Gruyter.

Smith, N. 1996. "The Production of Nature." In *Future Natural: Nature, Science, Culture*, edited by G. Robertson, M. Mash, L. Tickner, J. Bird, B. Curtis, and T. Putnam. New York: Routledge.

Sokal, Alan D. 1996. "Transgressing the Boundaries: Towards a Transformative Hermeneutics of Quantum Gravity." *Social Text* 46–47 (Spring–Summer): 217–52.

Soper, K. 1996. "Nature/'Nature.'" In *Future Natural: Nature, Science, Culture*, edited by G. Robertson, M. Mash, L. Tickner, J. Bird, B. Curtis, and T. Putnam. New York: Routledge.

Stanford, Richard. 2001. "Residing with Death." Ph.D. dissertation, University of New South Wales, Sydney.

Starobinski, Jean. 1979. *Words upon Words: The Anagrams of Ferdinand de Saussure*. Translated by O. Emmet. New Haven: Yale University Press.

Stern, Daniel. N. 2000. *The Interpersonal World of the Infant: A View from Psychoanalysis and Developmental Psychology*. New York: Basic Books.

Taylor, Mark C. 2001. *The Moment of Complexity: Emerging Network Culture.* Chicago: University of Chicago Press.

Ulmer, Gregory L. 1985. *Applied Grammatology: Post(e)-Pedagogy from Jacques Derrida to Joseph Beuys (E-Pedagogy from Jacques Derrida to Joseph Beuys).* Baltimore: Johns Hopkins University Press.

Uman, Martin. A. 1986. *All about Lightning.* New York: Dovers.

Wells, Gary. L. 1984. "How Adequate Is Human Intuition for Judging Eyewitness Testimony?" In *Eyewitness Testimony: Psychological Perspectives,* edited by G. L. Wells and E. F. Loftus. Cambridge: Cambridge University Press.

Wheeler, Wendy. 2006. *The Whole Creature: Complexity, Biosemiotics and the Evolution of Culture.* London: Lawrence and Wishart.

Whorf, Benjamin Lee. 1956. *Language, Mind and Reality: Selected Writings of Benjamin Lee Whorf.* Edited by J. B. Carroll. New York: MIT Press.

Wigner, Eugene P. 1960. "The Unreasonable Effectiveness of Mathematics in the Natural Sciences." *Communications on Pure and Applied Mathematics* 13:1–14.

Wilson, Elizabeth. A. 1998. *Neural Geographies: Feminism and the Microstructure of Cognition.* New York: Routledge.

———. 1999. "Introduction: Somatic Compliance—Feminism, Biology and Science." *Australian Feminist Studies* 14 (29): 7–18.

Index

Actor-network theory, 80
agency: distributed, 84–85, 87–89; entangled, x, 10, 98, 133; human, 71, 77, 79, 82
Anthropocentrism. *See* Humanism
Anthropomorphism, 87

Barad, Karen: on materiality and signification, 96, 146 n. 10; quantum entanglement, xi, 76, 133, 136, 149 n. 7, 151 n. 7, 154 n. 3; on the two-slit experiment, 126–27
Bennington, Geoffrey, 2
Biology, vii, 8, 65–66, 73, 75, 79, 93–94, 99, 100, 105, 146 n. 8, 149 n. 4, 152 n. 9
bodily ego, 103–6
Bohr, Niels, 126, 136, 151 n. 7
Butler, Judith: interview with, 72–74, 93; on nature/culture binary, 83–84, 87, 93–110, 151 n. 5; on signification, 78

Cartesianism, 14, 69–71, 74–75, 85, 91
causality: deconstruction and, 1, 3, 141 n. 7; locality and, 10–12, 25–27, 38, 58, 76, 126, 149 n. 8; scientific explanations of, ix, 49, 76–77

Changeux, Jean-Pierre, 66, 145 n. 5
Charcot, Jean-Martin, 65
chiasm, 94, 96–97, 109, 117, 120–21, 123, 134, 136, 151 n. 5, 154 n. 3
communication, 7–8, 10, 13, 19, 29, 32, 37, 58, 72, 76, 81–88, 92, 145 n. 6, 148 n. 1
Connes, Alain, 66, 145 n. 5
corporeality, ix, 27–29, 55, 63–64, 71, 74, 99, 104, 111, 114, 116–17, 120, 124, 128, 133
craniometry, 24–26
cultural criticism, 2, 91, 96
cultural constructionism, 3, 48, 72, 79, 82, 86, 93, 97, 98
Culture, 3, 14, 28, 31, 46, 49, 57, 78, 92, 101. *See also* nature/culture binary
cybernetics, 8

Dastur, Françoise, 114, 136
Derrida, Jacques: deconstruction, vii–xii, 1–21, 46, 113, 134, 149 n. 3, 152 n. 9; grammatology as science, 6–8, 59, 67, 73, 149 n. 6; speech/writing dichotomy, 54, 57, 61, 128, 147 n. 11
Devlin, Keith, 50, 65–66
dispositif, 81, 84–85, 151 n. 6

VICKI KIRBY IS AN ASSOCIATE PROFESSOR
in the School of Social Sciences and International
Studies at the University of New South Wales. She is
the author of *Judith Butler: Live Theory* (2006) and
Telling Flesh: The Substance of the Corporeal (1997).

LIBRARY OF CONGRESS
CATALOGING-IN-PUBLICATION DATA

Kirby, Vicki, 1950-
Quantum anthropologies : life at large / Vicki Kirby.
p. cm.
Includes bibliographical references and index.
ISBN 978-0-8223-5055-2 (cloth : alk. paper)
ISBN 978-0-8223-5073-6 (pbk. : alk. paper)
1. Feminist theory.
2. Politics and culture.
3. Culture—Philosophy. I. Title.
HQ1190.K573 2011
306.01—dc22   2011015608